# The Complete Works of Pat Parker

# The Complete Works of Pat Parker

## Edited by Julie R. Enszer

sapphic classics from
A MIDSUMMER NIGHT'S PRESS
& SINISTER WISDOM

*The Complete Works of Pat Parker,* edited by Julie R. Enszer

Poems copyright © 2016 by Anastasia Dunham-Parker-Brady.
All rights reserved.

A Midsummer Night's Press
amidsummernightspress@gmail.com
www.amidsummernightspress.com

Sinister Wisdom, Inc.
2333 Mcintosh Road
Dover, FL 33527
sinisterwisdom@gmail.com
www.sinisterwisdom.org

Designed by Nieves Guerra.

Cover photo © 2016 JEB (Joan E. Biren). Used with permission.
Title page drawing first appeared in *Child of Myself*.

First edition, October 2016
2nd printing, January 2018

ISBN-13 (Paperback): 978-1-938334-22-1
ISBN-13 (Hard Cover): 978-1-938334-32-0

Simultaneously published as *Sinister Wisdom* 102, ISSN: 0196-1853.

Printed in the U.S. on recycled paper.

# Contents

# Coming On Strong:
# A Legacy of Pat Parker
### By Judy Grahn

In her writing Pat Parker developed a fully authentic and revolutionary voice grounded in her experiences growing up Black and female in south Texas of the 1940s, and coming out as a lesbian/dyke in California of the late 1960s. The power of her poetry was profoundly fueled by three murders that directly impacted her life. Of course, all the usual harassments, injuries, insults, deprivations, husband abuses, exotifications and objectifications, heaped on Black women especially, came her way. The terror of being publically Gay, of losing community support as a person of color, of being misunderstood by her parents, also came her way. But I would say the murders pushed her over some edge of motivation to either withdraw completely or go to the front of the line with a big bad sword in hand and lead a revolution. This latter is what she did.

Parker and I were intensely collaborative poet comrades for ten years, from 1970-1980, then went separate ways for a while, and reunited in the late 1980s. We were reading to women-only audiences together by 1970; we traveled to venues, shared beds and adventures, and had many discussions about writing and politics, the overlaps and differences of our lives and the movements for which we had become public voices. I edited, typeset, helped design, printed, and assembled two of her books for the Women's Press Collective, which I co-founded in 1970 with the artist Wendy Cadden; I also edited Pat's collection *Movement in Black*, for Diana Press. Pat spoke in behalf of the Women's Press but never participated in its workings, saying that as the daughter of a father whose business was retreading tires, she had had enough of dirty jobs. She wanted something very different for herself.

Living in Houston during the 1940s, and despite cramped living quarters and scarce resources (see the story "Mama and the Hogs" in this volume) or "soul-searing poverty," as she said, Parker's family, the Cooks, had an optimistic spirit, belief in the power of education, and high expectations for the success of their children. The Texas they lived in, "Texas Hell," she called it, was a combination of oppressive conditions produced by white supremacy, and also pride in accomplishments of African-Americans--a combination of old dangers and new hopes that would require enormous courage and engagement with social movements for change to hold still long enough to include her.

Before she left home, two devastating killings had occurred, one of them her Uncle Dave; her mother insisted his death in jail was no suicide, no matter what the police said.

She spoke about the second murder in an interview with Anita Cornwell in 1975, first published in *Hera:*

> As a child in Texas, our newspaper boy was a faggot and he was killed by other kids in the community. They beat him up one night and threw him in front of a car. And everybody shook their heads and said how sad it was, but before then everybody had talked about how *strange* he was. So those kids were able to get away with killing him because the community just felt that it was sad, but he was a faggot, right? (from Part IV, interview with Anita Cornwell in 1975.)

When she was fresh out of high school at seventeen, Pat's family told her to get out of Houston, that she too could be killed. At the same time, Parker's teachers encouraged her to continue in school, and thought that she should become a lawyer in behalf of civil rights for Black people. According to one of her woman lovers, Parker's family, while living in reduced circumstances, nevertheless gave her a classical sense of education; for example they "loved all things ancient Greek."

Around 1973 Pat gave me her much-worn copy of John Ciardi's book on poetry techniques, *How Does a Poem Mean?,* as she said she would not need it any more. Both of us had studied his book in our early development as poets—she gave me her much-used copy not only because I had lost mine, but also as a statement that she did not need to work in formal English poetic styles any more: she had found her voice in the free verse, direct personal diction of Don L. Lee (Haki Madhubuti) who had decided that using metaphors enabled readers to avoid the real subject (of oppression, for example). Rhythm, irony, questions, repetition for emphasis, dramatic endings, humor, and story would become the architectural elements of Pat's poetry. She would open out that architecture for both ease of access and as a drum-call for activism.

Pat's quest for knowledge included a respect for forms, precise diction, emphatic idea of content. The voice she chose for her poetry held an unwavering moral compass that would lead members of her community audience to call her "Preacher." She was also a teacher dedicated to instructing her audience in what she had learned about life, oppression, justice, and intersectionality. I need to say here that four, at least, of us feminist poets—Parker, Audre Lorde, Adrienne Rich, and me—who were broadly and intensively formative of ideas in the 1970s and beyond, wrote of the intersections of our lives in ways that would later inform what continues to evolve in the academy and within social movements as "intersectionality."

Parker's teaching voice, while righteous and fired by outrage, was also meticulous and patient. In "For the White Person Who Wants to Be My Friend," she offers advice, basically: don't put me in a box called "black people are such and such" while at the same time, don't ever forget my vulnerability in a racist society.

For the younger women who in the 1980s began engaging in S/M practices she scolds with astonished questions: "Is this why we did it? / Did we grapple with our own who hated us/so women could use whips and chains?" And for her masterpiece, "Jonestown," she used the voice of a careful yet passionate lawyer, emphasizing her argument step by step about the enervating affects of American racism that can, did, and do still lead to mass murder with the apparent complicity of the victims.

Though she increasingly turned to rhythmic structures to frame her thoughts, her metaphors are also interesting. To explore a couple of them, for instance "chains" turns in her hands from heavy metal loops dragging on prisoners to bureaucratic paperwork to plastic credit cards to alienation among allies.

Another metaphor, addressed in "Poem to My Mother" in a very personal and ongoing argument of how religion has separated them, because of Pat's gayness:

You lied-
or made mistakes,
the difference - none
to the heart that raced
like a vehicle of my generation.

This was part of an extended plea for understanding between the generations: "Can you hear my tears? / each weighted by innards." Innards. Now there is an image to catch the breath.

I'm aware we now live in a society that has become very precious and finicky about its chicken, serving almost entirely white meat as "nuggets," "breast filets," or "tenders," all without bones, let alone feet or organs. So I certainly do want to speak to Pat's use of the image "innards" and its implication of steamy, variegated, throbbingly alive and extremely vulnerable inner self.

Innards. This reminds me of Parker's special meal, eaten occasionally and usually by herself, consisting of chicken hearts and gizzards, which she cooked up into a rubbery grey mass and doused with bright red Louisiana hot sauce; a sentimental if not ritual meal from her childhood. I believe she told me this was a favorite dish of her father's.

What do innards do, and hold? This seems important to unraveling Parker's deeper meanings. The gizzard processes whatever life offers, and the heart retains feeling and expresses. The guts—as in the chitterlings (hog intestines) she ate as soul food that "connects me to my ancestors" as she said in one poem—hold intuition as well as will and courage.

The metaphor of innards in Pat's poetry recurs with more than one meaning: "my innards...are twisted/ & torn & sectioned" in "My Hands are Big." She's explaining that her ideas and passion come from her family and its history, not from some easier-to-come-by political polemic that she has learned later in life. She is writing from her own direct experience, and also her family's, therefore from "innards," and understanding that these tightly held feelings, like her experiences, are "sectioned."

She used the image again twice in "Womanslaughter," her account of the third murder that impacted her life, the shooting death of her sister Shirley at the jealous hands of her ex-brother-in-law. Black on black crime of any sort was not taken seriously in the courts at that time, nor was what we would now call femicide.

> It doesn't hurt as much now
> the thought of you dead
> doesn't rip at my innards,
> leaves no holes to suck rage.

Holes in the innards, holes in the heart "suck rage." She turns that rage into a promise to become strong, to gather other strong women in solidarity:

> I will come with my many sisters
> and decorate the streets
> with the innards of those
> brothers in womenslaughter.

This threat, while emboldening to those working to end femicide in all its forms, and who are aware that strong female community works best for this, nevertheless has also not yet been addressed. To "decorate the streets" meaning not only the obvious but also to turn the perpetrators inside out, to read entrails (or innards) for motive and other truths. We know stories of countless victims, but the inner workings of the murderers and how to recognize and interrupt the patterns of male on female violence is far less known, far from understood and acted upon. The institutional support for their crimes has not yet been successfully challenged, and men are only beginning to answer the question "why?"

The three murders, then, as I see this, substantiate three oppressions that Pat took on to battle directly with her warrior voice: the first a product of white supremacy, and the continual murder of Black men especially, at the hands of the police. The second murder was from her own community (though it could have been nearly anyone's community—see the films *Brokeback Mountain* or *Boys Don't Cry* or *Two Spirits,*) almost casually getting rid of the *strange*—the Gay or Transgender or Two Spirit person. The third murder was femicide, directly experienced as the death of one of her beloved sisters.

At some point, perhaps with "Questions" and its refrain, "how do I break your chains?" as well as these lines: "now I'm tired/now you listen!/I have a dream too," her poetry went from explaining and depicting to mobilizing. By 1976 she had written "Movement in Black," a triumphant call for African-American women to move forward into leadership. The drum is a very effective instrument for mobilizing people. By shifting her poetic into rhythmic structures coupled with real life experience, Pat produced an amazing emphasis that was irresistible—a drum-call to action and activism, that goes straight to the heart with its own drumbeats, goes, one could say, directly for the "innards" as well as to the minds of the recipients.

Pat and I used to talk about how some people seemed to think we working class, or nonacademic poets just plucked our stuff effortlessly out of the air. "They don't realize how much study we have put into learning our craft," Pat said and I agreed people did not seem to see how much intense thought, feeling and structure we put into each poem. As our audiences became more enthusiastic (and we both had more than one community cheering us on) we increasingly crafted our work to be read aloud, and to be understood on the first hearing. This requires a kind of stanza by stanza pungency, that can and frequently did lead to dismissal from the more academic critics, especially early on, and especially for Pat, as she increasingly used repetition to drive her points home. We were aiming for the hearts and guts in our audiences, for the "innards." This isn't to say there is anything less poetic about denser, linguistically dexterous poetry, or poetry meant to evoke a scene or meditative feeling or brain spark. Just that orally-oriented poetry is a different exercise for different purposes, and that all art needs to be asked, among other questions, for what purpose were you crafted? What communities do you feed?

In the same spirit, and always with a big grin, Pat also liked to speak of the two of us as "poet athletes;" we were proud that we had muscles as well as brains and heart. She wanted, and achieved despite her life being cut short at the age of 45, a very full life, of family, of international politics, of sports, of art, of fulfilling work, and of leadership that continues through her poetic voice.

On a visit with Pat to her sister's suburban home in LA, her brother-in-law invited us to view his paintings in the studio he had built in the garage, and to let us know he was successful at selling his work. I saw how she admired their way of life as an achievement of both solidity and artfulness. "You see how they are doing this?" Pat said later to me, "It's really possible to have both security and creativity. " That was what she wanted. She had also wanted to be a different kind of poet, to indulge aesthetics and a variety of subjects, rather than constantly to be called (from within) to confront social aggressions in behalf of communities. Yet she also found profound meaning in the effects her work had on others.

In an interview she did with Pippa Fleming, who co-founded and served as editor for *Ache: A Journal for Black Lesbians*, Pat said this:

> If I died tomorrow and what could be said about my life is 'yes, she wrote books and she wrote poetry and people liked it,' that would not be enough. That's not why I take the risks that I do. A woman wrote a letter to me and the most touching things she said was, 'I'm doing my work so you don't have to do it for me.' What she's telling me by this is long after I'm gone, there are going to be women who will continue to do the work.

The great-hearted organizer Avotcja Jiltonilro, who combines her own poetry with dynamic live music, opened for Parker's gigs the last three years of her life, and then established a yearly memorial reading and performance evening celebrating Pat's birthday. This event in Berkeley helped raise money for Pat's life partner, Marty Dunham, in behalf of the college education fund for their daughter, Anastasia Dunham-Parker-Brady.

Both historic and prophetic, both contemporary and timelessly accessible, Pat Parker's voice will continue to influence as we all go forward into new challenges and opportunities to lead meaningful lives.

# Movement in Black

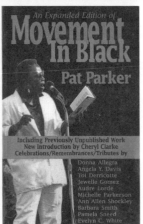

# Foreword

On the last night of my first trip to the West Coast in 1969, I walked into a room and met a young Black poet with fire in her eyes, a beer in her hand and a smile/scowl on her face. There were poems in her mouth, on the tables, in the refrigerator, under the bed, and in the way she cast about the apartment, searing for—not answers—but rather, unexpressable questions. We were both Black; we were Lesbians; we were both poets, in a very white, straight, male world, and we sat up all night trading poems. The next day the continent divided us, and during the next few years I read Pat Parker's two earlier books with appreciation, sometimes worrying about whether or not she'd/we'd survive. (Which for Black/Poet/Women is synonymous with grow).

Now, with love and admiration, I introduce Pat Parker and this new collection of her poetry. These poems would not need any introduction except for the racism and heterosexism of a poetry establishment which has whited out Parker from the recognition deserved by a dynamic and original voice in our poetry today.

> I am a child of America
> a step child
>     raised in a back room

Even when a line falters, Parker's poetry maintains, reaches out and does not let go. It is clean and sharp without ever being neat. Yet her images are precise, and the plain accuracy of her visions encourages an honesty that may be uncomfortable as it is compelling. Her words are womanly and uncompromising.

> SISTER! your foot's smaller
> but it's still on my neck.

Her tenderness is very direct:

> A woman's body must be taught to speak
> bearing a lifetime of keys, a patient soul

and her directness can be equally tender:

> My hands are big
> and rough and callous
> like my mother's—

Her Black Woman's voice rings true and deep and gentle, with an iron echo. It is merciless and vulnerable and far ranging. In her poems Parker owns her weaknesses and she owns her strengths, and she does not give up. Even when she weeps, her words evoke that real power which is core-born.

> A pit is an abyss
> let's drink to my shame

For as a Black Lesbian poet Parker knows, that for all women, the most enduring conflicts are far from simple.

And for the Sisters who still think that fear is a reason to be silent, Parker's poetry says loudly and clearly: I HAVE SURVIVED! I SEE, AND I SPEAK!

Audre Lorde

# MARRIED

Drawing by Wendy Cadden. Used with permission

# Goat Child

## I. 1944-1956

"you were a mistake"
my mother told me
ever since i've been
trying to make up.
couldn't really imagine
her/him in bed &
me coming 4 years after
the last sister
& to make things worse
i come blasting in
2 months too soon.
maybe the war did it
& to top the whole thing off
i'm the fourth girl
& my father was pissed.
caught pneumonia &
got hung up in [an] incubator
for three months
finally made it out,
but the bed was too big
so my sister lost her doll bed.
another enemy quickly made.
& my old man being typical
spade businessman
too much credit – too little capital
loses his shop, &
we move to what is now
suburbs of Houston only
it had weeds and space
move to our own home
away from two-story brick
project where i found my
cousin's condom & blew it up
& good-bye cousins to

one room – tin roof playhouse
with tarzan making beams,
tin #2 washtub, maggot-filled
outhouse and super rats /
but i did try to please then.
football, baseball, fishing,
best yard cutter on the block.
two guns hanging from my hips
in the best Texas tradition
& me bad pistol pete holding
up all visitors for nickels
& wiping out roaches faster
than the durango kid ever could.
but even the best cowboys need learning
so they herded me back to school
but i remembered nursery school
& nurses with long needles
hell no i won't go,
but i went & had to leave
my guns/could only take
my boots & the teacher
300 lbs. of don'ts
& i cried thru a whole day
of turtles, lizards, pretty
pictures, crayons, & glue.
came back all ready to
hang up the second day,
but the teacher showed
us her paddle – heavy
wood, hand fitted paddle
with holes drilled to
suck the flesh/no tears
so i settled down &
fought my way thru first grade
defending my right to
wear cowboy boots even if
i was a girl which no one

had bothered to tell me
about at home / swung
into 2nd grade right into
economics / 50¢ notebook
which mother couldn't
buy that day & i couldn't
tell the teacher that rap
so i copped one from the
doctor's son who could
afford it easy, but he
had numbered his pages
& i couldn't explain why
my book began on pg. 9
& the teacher calls
my sister who has been
her star #1 pupil
four years ago who
immediately denies that
her mother had bought it
& there i was caught
thief at seven years old.
conditions improved /
looked like i was going
to make it till 5th grade
& i got beat all day
for stealing a 15¢ pack
of paper which i didn't,
but couldn't say because the
girl that did was too big
& the teacher got religion
& bought me steak sandwiches
from then on & even put me
in the glee club which was
indeed a most generous act.
& 6th grade was worse cause
oldest sister #2 had been
there and & the teacher had

a good memory for bad ones.
& it wasn't until
i recited the night
before christmas
three times on our
class program that
she forgave me.

**II.**

the goat left this child
me still trying to butt
my way in or out
& i came home dripping
blood & panic rode in
on my shoulders.
her slipped to the store
returned clutching a
box of kotex in a sack
twice as large.
"now you can have babies,
so keep your panties up"
& i couldn't see the
connection between me &
babies cause i wasn't
even thinking of marriage
& that always came first.
& him having to admit that
i really was a girl &
all of a sudden no more
football, not even touch
or anything & now getting
angry because i still
didn't like dolls &
all this time me not knowing
that the real hang up
was something called virginity

which i had already lost
2 years ago to a really
hard-up rapist that i
never could tell my parents
about, not really knowing what
had happened but somehow
feeling it would not be
to my advantage.
twelve years old
& in a southern Baptist
tradition that meant
the leaving of childhood
& the latest acceptable
time to go to God
so with pleas of the
family image ringing
in my ears / i went
baptism / no evil spirit
left / just cold & wet
waiting to be struck
down for fraud
& now mickey – a
baptism present to
replace delmonte
who replaced scotty
who replaced queen
who went mad and
ran thru the streets
foaming with me
climbing fences to
cut her off at the pass
but mickey a pup
already at my knees
orange, blue-tongued
chow who ate on his
trainer who played with
his food and him brings

the victor to me/
scared but even more
afraid of it being
known & mickey just
as afraid as me, but
we learned and i
unchained him &
took the christmas
bike and rode free
miles and miles
& mickey running
ahead challenging
anyone or dog to
get too close.
the goat came charging back
& my sisters could no
longer tell me
& the fights won in the day
lost when him came
at night, but renewed
each day with each new welt
& the boys at school
learned that him was crazy
& off to the jr. prom
with the faggot in the
church choir/ the only
acceptable male other
than him & the hate
chickens, ducks &
rabbits who ate their
young when i forgot
to put in more salt and
beating and the volleyball
team i almost made varsity
but the gym floor & stitches
& better grades to apologize
pajama parties & mothers

who knew to go to bed
dirty jokes that i
didn't quite understand
& beer and drunkenness
the friend who always
imitated me clomping
the cha cha & never
saw my pain/ horns
shrank until senior
year & debate champion
who really want to
write but more afraid
of the coach who
knew i was the next
great spade lawyer
& failed the only
boy i ever loved to
make sure i didn't
get married/ her
pissed because i didn't get the
scholarship/ the big one
me who never told of
the little one that
would have kept me
in texas/ new pastures
for the goat.
     OUT
run to california
& golden streets
& big money
& freedom to go
anywhere & not being
served in new mexico
or arizona/ not stopping
to record that &
california streets
reeked of past glories

and wine and blood
and this brave young
goat blasting full
steam into everything
breaking into the landlady's
window while showing
a young delinquent
a backhand & running
like hell, laughing
till it hurt &
his ole lady was
paying me to keep him out
of trouble.
college and the german
who didn't want me
to know his language
& decided maybe adolph
wasn't so great after
all.
journalism
a friend who
cut her forearms
to commit suicide
& me offering to help
her do it right
& retired lady colonel
who didn't think i
liked her class &
this young beast
emphatically affirmed
her / journalism "C"
a little dark buddha
walked in with folder
"i'd like to see more
of your writing"/ me
awed – a man – who
knew about the goat.

### III. 1962-1966

"i am a man,"
the buddha said —
come with me &
i will show you
the ways of woman.
come with me &
i will show you
the world of being —
the world of pain
the world of joy
the world of hate
the world of love
come walk with me
i will show you
why? — you are.
this goat child charged
muscles tensed,
leaped, trampled
into a new time
a time of talk
a time of wine
parties & me
not knowing the words,
the gestures,
not knowing
history or heritage,
not knowing
the liars or their lies,
but sensing, somewhere.
my head — hooded,
allowed to breathe,
but not to see —
a blind goat charging
"i am a man,"
the buddha said

"come with me &
i will show you
the ways of woman."
this goat saw & felt
the blood run,
leave my body –
i could not find the eyes,
no heart, no limbs
only blood, deep dark
blood that was life
that was dead –
scraped away
with a surgeon's knife.
scraped into regret
scraped into pain
non-existent
but real,      real!
and the herds
herds of goats
herds of sheep
& the shepherds –
give me your milk
give me your wool
& we will feed you
we will protect you
the shepherds came
& taught me skills
to provide for them.
"come with me &
i will show you
the ways of woman"
& i learned
i learned hate
i learned jealousy
i learned my skills –
to cook – to fuck
to wash – to fuck

to iron – to fuck
to clean – to fuck
to care – to fuck
to wait – to fuck
& this goat-child cried
& screamed & ran
& the buddha's smile left
& his wisdom faded
& his throne crumbled
& the buddha left &
returned a shepherd.
in that leaving
the goat-child died –
the goat-child died
& a woman was born.

# For Donna

Somewhere you live
and i
am many years          away,
no longer a frightened child
capable only of giving birth.

i wonder of your mother

not me —

      for i have never washed you
              never fed you
              never touched you.

If she tells you of me
will you understand?

understand my choice =
give away part of myself
             to save part of myself

If she tells you of me,

will you hate me?

      i know hate.
      i know the hate of your father,
      i know that hate of the mothers —
           who kept their children,

i will accept your hate

but my child

you can never hate me

as much as i have hated myself.

Sometimes my husband
acts
just like a man...


dishes are evil / you know
they can destroy the spirit...

Washing dishes should
be outlawed

paper plate nirvana!

long live dixie cups!

     ...tomorrow i am going to lose
     my temper –

     i will destroy all the dishes
     that i missed last week –

# Fuller Brush Day

Here you are, lady,
a year's supply of room spray,
& I watch myself
walking down
my hall,
spraying for a year.
Spraying for a year,
spray here – spray there
walking down my hall
spraying room spray,
an artificial forest
wiping out city smells.
Artificial forest,
minus birds
minus squirrels,
minus dew
minus –
spraying for a year.

If you run out before
a year's time
we'll give you another bottle
Another bottle
a full
definite
permanent year's bottle

permanent year
365 ¼ days
no time given
to holidays
one year,
spray for a year
phony forest
for a year

forest in my kitchen
forest in my toilet
forest in my cat box
a full time
real life forest
smelling type year.
Walking down my halls
spraying for a year
365 ¼ days
of spray
spray
spray
& I bought it.

To see a man cry –
is like watching animals
in a zoo,
  say
the baby elephant
      whose trunk is
            too short
            or my arm
isn't long enough
and the peanuts
won't quite reach
            but fall among husks
like your tears
            mating with mine
  in frustration.

Even in our worst times
some part of us –
finds each other.

# You can't be sure of anything these days

You meet a really far-out man –
tells you,
he's been on his own for years
   opens car doors for you
   carries packages for you
   protects you from evil-doers
says he wants an intelligent, creative
   woman to be his *partner* in life.

       you marry and find
the dude is
    too weak to pick up a dish
    too dumb to turn on a burner
    too afraid to do laundry
    too tense to iron a shirt
& to top the whole thing off –
he tries to cover his incompetence
by telling YOU –
     it's women's work.

You can't be sure of anything these days.

# Exodus
## (To my husbands, lovers)

*a going out or going forth;*
*departure.*

Trust me no more –
Our bed is unsafe.
Hidden within folds of cloth
a cancerous rage –

i will serve you no more
in the name of wifely love
i'll not masturbate your pride
in the name of wifely loyalty.

Trust me no more
Our bed is unsafe
Hidden within folds of cloth
a desperate slave

You dare to dismiss my anger
        call it woman's logic
You dare to claim my body
        call it wifely duty.

Trust me no more
Your bed is unsafe
Rising from folds of cloth –

# A Moment Left Behind

Have you ever tried to catch a tear?
Catch it on bent fingers.
Press it against eyelids,
And wish the moment.

Or capture bitter words
Ripped from your throat like timber
And surround them –
islands of instant.

I do not claim all possible
Creating myths of modern America.
I cannot swim an ocean.
I attempt the width of a pool.

# From Deep Within

Nature tests those she would calls hers;
Slips up, naked and blank down dark paths.
Skeletons of the sea, this we would become
to suck a ray of sight from the fire.

A woman's body must be taught to speak —
Bearing a lifetime of keys, a patient soul,
moves through a maze of fear and bolts
clothed in soft hues and many candles.

The season's tongues must be heard & taken,
And many paths built for the travelers.
A woman's flesh learns slow by fire and pestle,
Like succulent meats, it must be sucked and eaten.

# LIBERATION FRONTS

My hands are big
and rough & callused –
like my mother's.

My innards are twisted
and torn and sectioned –
like my father's.

Now - some of
my sisters see me
        as big & twisted
            rough & torn
            callused & sectioned
definitely not pleasant,
to be around –


I.


Had i listened to my father

i would be
married & miserable
        dreaming of fish
        & open space
        & bellowing my needs –
                waiting for some one
                to listen to the second run
                & know –

it is difficult to be
        strong –
        & appear sure
no one ever believes
when you cry.

**II.**

Had i listened to my mother
i would be married & miserable
    dreaming – praying
    of security
& choking on my needs
    waiting for someone
    to listen to the second run
    & know

It is difficult to be
    quiet –
    & appear sure
no one believes
when you
  don't
show your tears.

**III.**

My hands are big & rough
    like my mother's
my innards are twisted & torn
    like my father's
my self is
    my big hands –
        like my father's
& torn innards –
        like my mother's
& they both felt
& were
& i am a product of that –
& not a political consciousness

*This at last is bone of my bones*
        *and flesh of my flesh;*
she shall be called Woman,
    because she was taken out of
Man.
                        Genesis 2:23


from cavities of bones
spun
        from caverns of air
i, woman – bred of man
taken from the womb of sleep;
i, woman that comes
before the first.

to think second
to believe first
        a mistake
        erased by the motion of years.
i, woman, i
 can no longer claim
        a mother of flesh
        a father of marrow
I, Woman, must be
        the child of myself.

*There are two things I've got a*
*right to, and these are death*
*or liberty. One or the other*
*i mean to have.*
Harriet Tubman

Brother
        I don't want to hear
        about
        how *my* real enemy
        is the system.
i'm no genius,
        but i do know
        that system
you hit me with
        is called
            a fist.

*How do we know that the panthers*
*will accept a gift from*
*white – middle – class – women?*


Have you ever tried to hide?
        In a group
                of women
                        hide
        yourself
slide between the floor boards
slide yourself away child
        away from this room
                & your sister
before she notices
        your Black self &
her white mind
                slide your eyes
                        down
away from the other Blacks
        afraid – a meeting of eyes
& pain would travel between you –
        change like milk to buttermilk
                a silent rage.
                        SISTER! your foot's smaller,
but it's still on my neck.

In English Lit.,
        they told me
Kafka was good
        because he created
the best nightmares ever –
I think I should
go find that professor
& ask why
we didn't study
the S.F. Police Dept.

My heart is fresh cement,
Still able to mark on,
but in short time,
No,
     I will not dry,
    covering the streets of men
                with hate

BLEW HOT SOUL SISTER
     My breath leaves me –
arid words crack,
     tumble, to the floor
like spilled salt.

Hate – Kill – hate – kill

That's primitive –

Yes, primitive,

    Be

Run naked thru jungles

    run
           run

wallow in trampled grass,

    trampled,

        run,

be, primitive

    like sex –

filthy,

    sweaty,    be

hate,

    my guts ache

KEEP your guns,

    or you die first    run

kill, hate, run

    killhaterundie

primitive/free

    hate    kill

NO!

    wet grass is sticky.

# Dialogue

Mother, dear mother, I'm dying,
People are frowning at me,
I spend my time now, crying,
I don't know what to be.

Child, dear child, I'm sad,
To know that you've gone astray,
Beatniks, you know, are bad,
I hope you find the way.

Mother, dear mother, I'm frightened,
They're dropping bombs about my head,
I'm afraid to bother to make a friend,
For I'm sure she'd wind up dead.

Child, dear child, you're silly,
The bombs are for the enemy,
And every good person is willing,
To help keep our country free.

Mother, dear mother, I'm passed,
Working my whole life away,
Trying to join a higher class,
and living in utter decay.

Child, dear child, I must, *
Show you the way to God,
First, you learn to trust,
& stop doing things that are odd.

Mother, dear mother, are you blind?
You've seen nothing I've said,
What will you do when you find,
Your child has fallen down dead?

Child, dear child, I'll buy,
A large casket made of gold,
I'll sit beside you and cry,
& pray to God for your soul.

With the sun –
fear leaves me
rushes to cover /
leaves lumps
like the backyard gopher
to remind me.

I am afraid
of anyone
of anything
that would harm me /
not the pain
not the act
but,
   the desire.

# For Michael on His Third Birthday

*"What are you, Michael?"*
*"Black and Beautiful."*

A distant time passed
Men chained back to back
Destined pain by cast
Slave – night men – Black

Overseers of then & tomorrow
Families born into a pack
Believing – that they borrow
Slaves – dead men – Black

Hurt – doubters of the lie
Death the only fact
Teach the son to die
Slaves – free men – Black

Slaves, dead, under ground
Fire swallows the rack
The gun has turned around
MEN – Beautiful and Black

# A Family Tree

*Cursed be Canaan;*
*a slave of slaves*
*shall he be to his*
*brothers.*
 Genesis 9:25 

Pitch sun-child drowns in the Mississippi,
washes away chains of loneliness, floats
a drum beat on the Nile.

Daughter of Ham lies on a church floor;
filled in orgasm with her Maker,
a spent lover ignorant of a hard bed.

The sperm of a million nights
sings loud over the southern skies;
– Sirens to a nation's conscience.

A babe of illusion has been born.
She will tell the world of rainbows;
And kiss the holes in its eyes.

# Sunday

Each Sunday
    the people    of this town
would go to church
    eat dinner
        all at one table with their family
    the television silent
        & bless the food,
           father
                we thank
                   THEE

    & their maids
off
    with their families
  & everyone rested
  until the Sunday
    when the rains
    began
        and crashed
        thru the wind
    moving away the dirt
    but somebody didn't
    stop it
        and the
little river
    rose
        and
            rose
till the cars
and televisions
and blankets
and people – all
washed through the
    streets and past
    their neighbors
    for blocks
        and blocks

The troops came on Wednesday
The water had
      stopped
   the wet
merged with the dirt
      mud
              was
      all over
              and
      the troops shook their heads.

They could not
      bury
      the dead.

In the
      death murk

they could not tell
      the
      Black
      from
      the white.

# Pied Piper

She sits,
ebony skinned,
drawing sun rays.
Children cluster;
a jagged circle
presses inward.
Sand-covered feet
Lean,
in homage to
the High Priestess.
The classical reed
will not suffice.

A Conga

Willowy notes
are not heard.
Deep, tense, beats
climb down the drum,
Jumping out in the air,
Lions roaring at children.

Conga

Black hands
beat the skin;
a white bred
with sweat.

Conga

Drum beats
dance over the waves,
& children's kayaks
drift inward.

The priestess rests.
Her fingers cuddle
the drum head.
Children query, with
eyes showing no hate,
"What kind of drum is it?"
"Conga"
"You play good;
Is it a message?"
"Message?"
"Yes, what does it mean?
What song is it?"

"It's a Mau Mau death song."

i wonder
how many matches
it would take,
to lay a single-file trail
from here –
to richard nixon's ass.

It's probably not a good idea.
I can see him now –
Waving his singed prick
on nation-wide television,
telling how it was saved
by a tub of confidence
provided by
his silent majority.

# Where do you go to become a non-citizen?

I want to resign; I want out.
I want to march to the nearest place
Give my letter to a smiling face.
I want to resign; I want out.

President Ford vetoed a jobs bill
Sent to him from capitol hill
While we sit by being super cool
He gets a $60, 000 swimming pool.
I wanna resign; I want out.

$68,000 to Queen Elizabeth to not grow cotton.
Yet there's no uproar that this jive is rotten.
$14,000 to Ford Motors to not plant wheat
I guess the government don't want wheat all over
        the seats.
I wanna resign; I want out.

The CIA Commission was in session for 26 weeks long
Said the boys didn't do too much wrong
They gave out acid – a test – they tell
Yet if you and I used it – we'd be in jail.
I wanna resign; I want out.

And from Taft College – a small group of fools
Chased all the Black students out of the school.
And good citizens worries about property sale
Chased away Black teenagers from picturesque Carmel.
I wanna resign; I want out.

The Little League after using all excuses up
Says a 10-year-old-girl must use a boy's supportive cup.
An international Women's Congress in Mexico to make plans
Elected for their president – a white-liberal man.
I wanna resign; I want out.

The A.P.A. finally said all gays aren't ill
Yet ain't no refunds on their psychiatry bills.
A federal judge says MCC is valid – a reality
Yet it won't keep the pigs from hurting you or me.
I wanna resign; I want out.

I wanna resign; I want out.
Please lead me to the place
Show me the smiling face
I'm skeptical – full of doubt.
I wanna resign; I want out.

*"Don't let the fascists speak."*
*"We want to hear what they have to say."*
*"Keep them out of the classroom."*
*"Everybody is entitled to freedom of speech."*

I am a child of America
a step child
     raised in the back room
yet taught
     taught how to act
in her front room.
my mind jumps
the voices of students
screaming
insults       threats
*"Let the Nazis speak"*
*"Let the Nazis speak"*
Everyone is entitled
     to speak
I sit a greasy-legged
     Black child
in a Black school
in the Black part of town
look to the Black teacher
*the Bill of Rights*
     guarantees
us all the right
     my mind
remembers   chants
article I       article I
& my innards churn
they remember
the Black teacher
in the Black school

in the Black part
of the very white town
who stopped us
when we attacked
the puppet principal
the white Board
of mis-Education
cast-off books
illustrated with
cartoons &
words of wisdom
written by white
children in the
other part of town
missing pages
caricatures
of hanging niggers –
*the bill of rights*
*was written to*
      *protect*
        *us*

my mind remembers
& my innards churn
conjures images
      police
break up
illegal demonstrations
illegal assemblies
      conjures images
of a Black Panther
*"if tricky Dick*
*tries to stop us*
*we'll stop him"*
conjure image
of that same Black man
going to jail

for threatening
the life of
      THE PRESIDENT
*every citizen*
*is entitled to*
*freedom of speech*
my mind remembers
& my innards churn
conjure images
of jews in camps
of homosexuals in camps
of socialists in camps
*"Let the Nazis speak"*
*"Let the Nazis speak"*
      faces in a college
            classroom
*"You're being fascist too."*
*"We want to hear what*
*they have to say"*

      faces in
a college classroom
young white faces
      speak let them speak
speak let them speak
Blacks, jews some whites
seize the bullhorn
*"We don't want to hear*
*your socialist rhetoric"*
      socialist rhetoric
      survival
                  rhetoric
the supreme court
says it is illegal
to scream fire
in a crowded theater

to scream fire
in a crowded theater
causes people to panic
to run to hurt each other
my mind remembers
& now i know
what my innards
        say
illegal to cause
        people
to panic
to run
to hurt
there is
no contradiction
what the Nazis say
will cause
        people
        to hurt
        ME.

# To My Vegetarian Friend

It's not called soul food
because it goes with music.
It is a survival food.

    from the grease
sprang generations
of my people
       generations
    of slaves
that ate the leavings
    of their masters
          & survived

And when I sit –
faced by
chitterlins & greens
neckbones & tails
it is a ritual –
it is a joining –
me to my ancestors
& your words ring untrue
this food is good for me
It replenishes my soul

so if you really
can't stand
to look at my food
can't stand
to smell my food
& can't keep those feelings
    to yourself

Do us both a favor
& stay home

# For the white person who wants to know how to be my friend

The first thing you do is to forget that i'm Black.
Second, you must never forget that i'm Black.

You should be able to dig Aretha,
but don't play her every time i come over.
And if you decide to play Beethoven – don't tell me
his life story. They made us take music appreciation too.

Eat soul food if you like it, but don't expect me
to locate your restaurants
or cook it for you.

And if some Black person insults you,
mugs you, rapes your sister, rapes you,
rips your house, or is just being an ass –
please, do not apologize to me
for wanting to do them bodily harm.
It makes me wonder if you're foolish.

And even if you really believe Blacks are better lovers than
whites – don't tell me. I start thinking of charging stud fees.

In other words – if you really want to be my friend – *don't*
make a labor of it. I'm lazy. Remember.

Tour America!
a T.V. commercial said.
I will –
there are things I need:
    travelers checks in new york
    gas mask in Berkeley
    face mask in Los Angeles
National guardsmen to protect me
    – in the south
Marines to protect me
    from guardsmen
    – in the mid-west,
Police to protect me
    from hustlers
    – in the ghettos,
Bullet-proof vest and helmet
    to protect me from police
    – everywhere.

Tour America!
perhaps,
    it would be better

to blow it up.

I'm so tired
of hearing about
    capitalist
    sexist,
    racist,
    fascist
    chauvinist,
    feminist.

I am tired
of hearing about
    confronting
    demonstrating
    trashing,
    smashing,
    surviving,
    jiving.

I'm beginning to
wonder if
the tactics
of this revolution
 is to
talk the enemy to death.

# The *What* Liberation Front?

Today i had a talk with my dog
he called me a racist – chauvinist person
told me he didn't like the way
i keep trying to change him.
Dogs – he said – do not shit in toilets
Dogs – like to shit outside & he didn't
appreciate being told to shit in the gutter –
just because i didn't like the smell of his shit –
he informed me that the fish weren't so hot
about my shit either.
& property – he wanted to know why
people expected dogs to protect their capitalist interest
he never watches television or plays
records. & how come i put tags on him.
My dog – he laughed. He is his own dog.
And what's this bullshit about his sex
life. If he wants to fuck in the streets it's
his business & the genocide against dogs –
now by this time he's growling – & i just
said – he didn't have to get nasty – i was
willing to study the problem. After all didn't
i buy him good bones and get him groomed
once a month & then he starts hollering
about if he wanted to get dirty &
have long hair that was his right too.
And another thing he said – if he wants to
sit he'll sit – so just shovel my shit about
sit, lie, roll over, stand up. And finally
he said standing up – the next time i patted
him on the head & called him a good boy
he was gonna lift his leg – With that,
he got up & left the house saying something
about a consciousness-raising meeting.

# Snatches of a Day

Grey clouds floated past my window –

    & I ignored them,
    danced into the streets,
    stoned on life.

A woman with brown hair

    like dirty corduroy,
    riding in a Malibu,
    with an olive green suit,
    & a big cigar
    stared at me.
I stopped dancing.

An old cripple dragged past me –

    I offered to carry her;
    She called me a nigger.
        I cut her throat,
        danced around her head,
        sang, "We Shall Overcome"
        hung her scalp over Woolworth's candy counter.

Cops started to arrest me.
    Said I couldn't dance without a permit.
    So, I skipped slowly.

Science teacher lectured for an hour,
    Never did tell me his name,
    So, I didn't tell him mine,
Just my student body & social security numbers.

A friend gave me a God's eye –
    Shocked me,
    Didn't know He had eyes.

My cousin died last week.
    He was a hero.
    Died defending my liberty –
    O sweet liberty,
    Land of the free
    & the great.

Went to a dull move.
Watched a guy masturbate.

I want to go to sleep.
My cat won't let me under the covers.

Boots are being polished
Trumpeters clean their horns
Chains and locks forged
The crusade has begun.

Once again flags of Christ
are unfurled in the dawn
and cries of soul saviors
sing apocalyptic on air waves.

Citizens, good citizens all
parade into voting booths
and in self-righteous sanctity
X away our right to life.

I do not believe as some
that the vote is an end.
I fear even more
It is just a beginning.

So I must make assessment
Look to you and ask:
Where will you be
when they come?


They will not come
a mob rolling
through the streets
but quickly and quietly
move into our homes
and remove the evil,
the queerness,
the faggotry,

the perverseness
from their midst.
They will not come
clothed in brown
and swastikas, or
bearing chests heavy   with
gleaming crosses.
The time and   need
for ruses are   over.
They will come
in business suits
to buy your homes
and bring bodies to
fill your jobs.
They will come in robes
to rehabilitate
and white coats
to subjugate
and where will you be
when they come?

Where will we *all be*
when they come?
And they will come –

they will come
because we are
defined as opposite –
perverse
and we are perverse.

Every time we watched
a queer hassled in the
streets and said nothing –
It was an act of perversion.

Every time we lied about
the boyfriend or girlfriend

at coffee break —
It was an act of perversion.

Every time we heard,
"I don't mind gays
but why must they
be blatant?" and said nothing —
It was an act of perversion.

Every time we let a lesbian mother
lose her child and did not fill
the courtrooms —
It was an act of perversion.

Every time we let straights
make out in bars while
we couldn't touch because
of laws —
It was an act of perversion.

Every time we put on the proper
clothes to go to a family
wedding and left our lovers
at home —
It was an act of perversion.

Every time we heard
"Who I go to bed with
is my personal choice —
it's personal not political"
and said nothing —
It was an act of perversion.

Every time we let our straight relatives
bury our dead and push our
lovers away —
It was an act of perversion.

And they will come.
They will come for
the perverts

& it won't matter
if you're
> homosexual, not a faggot
> lesbian, not a dyke
> gay, not queer

It won't matter
if you
> own your business
> have a good job
> or are on S.S.I.

It won't matter
if you're
> Black
> Chicano
> Native American
> Asian
> or White

It won't matter
if you're from
> New York
> or Los Angeles
> Galveston
> or Sioux Falls

It won't matter
if you're
> Butch, or Fem
> Not into roles
> Monogamous
> Non Monogamous

It won't matter
If you're
> Catholic

Baptist
Atheist
Jewish
or M.C.C.

They will come
They will come
to the cities
and to the land
to your front rooms
and in *your* closets.

They will come for
the perverts
and where will
you be
When they come?

# Questions

*"Until all oppressed people*
*are free –*
*none of us are free."*

**I.**

the chains are different now –
lay on this body strange
no metal clanging in my ears

chains laying strange
chains laying light-weight
laying credit cards
laying welfare forms
laying buying time
laying white packets of dope
laying afros & straightened hair
laying pimp & revolutionary
laying mother & daughter
laying father & son

chains laying strange –
strange laying chains
        chains

how do i break these chains

**II.**

the chains are different now –
laying on this body strange
funny chains – no clang
chains laying strange
chains laying light-weight
chains laying dishes
chains laying laundry

chains laying grocery markets
chains laying no voice
chains laying children
chains laying *selective* jobs
chains laying less pay
chains laying girls & women
chains laying wives & women
chains laying mothers & daughters

chains laying strange
strange laying chains
        chains

how do i break these chains

**III.**

the chains are still here
laying on this body strange
no metal – no clang
chains laying strange
chains laying light-weight
chains laying funny
chains laying different
chains laying dyke
chains laying bull-dagger
chains laying pervert
chains laying no jobs
chains laying more taxes
chains laying beatings
chains laying stares
chains laying myths
chains laying fear
chains laying revulsion

chains laying strange
strange laying chains
        chains

how do i break these chains

**IV.**

the chains are here
no metal – no clang
chains of ignorance & fear
chains here – causing pain

how do i break these chains
to whom or what
do i direct pain
>       Black – white
>       mother – father
>       sister – brother
>       straight – gay

how do i break these chains
how do i stop the pain
who do I ask – to see
what must i do – to be free

sisters – how do i break your chains
brothers – how do i break your chains
mothers – how do i break your chains
fathers – how do i break your chains

i don't want to kill –
i don't want to cause pain –

how –
how else do i break – your chains

i have a dream
 no –
 not Martin's
though my feet moved
 down many paths.
it's a simple dream –

i have a dream
 not the dream of the vanguard
 not to turn this world –
     all over
 not the dream of the masses
not the dream of women
     not to turn this world
       all
           over
it's a simple dream –

In my dream –
 i can walk the streets
   holding hands with my lover

In my dream –
 i can go to a hamburger stand
   & not be taunted by bikers on a holiday

In my dream –
 i can go to a public bathroom,
   & not be shrieked at my ladies –

In my dream –
 i can walk ghetto streets
   & not be beaten up by my brothers.

In my dream –
 i can walk out of a bar
   & not be arrested by the pigs

I've placed this body
      placed this mind
      in lots of dreams –
      in Martin's & Malcolm's –
      in Huey & Mao's –
      in George & Angela's –
      in the north & south
               of Vietnam & America
                     & Africa

i've placed this body & mind
      in dreams –
      dreams of people –

now i'm tired –
now you listen!
      i have a dream too.
      it's a simple dream.

# MOVEMENT IN BLACK

Pat Parker reading "Movement in Black" at Cal State/LA with her niece, two sisters, and the writer Ayofemi Stowe Folayan in March 1989

# Movement in Black

Movement in Black
movement in Black
can't keep em back
movement in Black

I.

They came in ships
from a distant land
bought in chains
to serve the man

I am the slave
that chose to die
I jumped overboard
& no one cried

I am the slave
sold as stock
walked to and fro
on the auction block

They can be taught
if you show them how
they're strong as bulls
and smarter than cows.

I worked in the kitchen
cooked ham and grits
seasoned all dishes
with a teaspoon of spit.

I worked in the fields
picked plenty of cotton
prayed every night
for the crop to be rotten.

All slaves weren't treacherous
that's a fact that's true
but those who were
were more than a few.

Movement in Black
Movement in Black
Can't keep em back
Movement in Black

II.

I  am the Black woman
& I have been all over
when the colonists
fought the British
i was there
i aided the colonist
i aided the British
i carried notes,
stole secrets,
guided the men
& nobody thought
to bother me
i was just a
Black woman
the britishers lost
and I lost,
but I was there
& I kept on moving

I am the Black woman
& i have been all over
i went out west, yeah
the Black soldiers
had women too,
& i settled the land,

& raised crops & children,
but that wasn't all

I hauled freight,
& carried mail,
drank plenty whiskey
shot a few men too.
books don't say much
about what I did
but I was there
& I kept on moving.

I am the Black woman
& i have been all over
up on platforms & stages
talking about freedom
freedom for Black folks
freedom for women
In the civil war too
carrying messages,
bandaging bodies
spying and lying
the south lost
& i still lost
but I was there
& i kept on moving

I am the Black woman
& I have been all over
I was on the bus
with Rosa Parks
& in the streets
with Martin King
I was marching
and singing
and crying
and praying

I was with SNCC
& i was with CORE
I was in Watts
when the streets
were burning
I was a panther
in Oakland
in new york
with N.O.W.
In San Francisco
with gay liberation
in D.C with
the radical dykes
yes, I was there
& i'm still moving

movement in Black
movement in Black
can't keep em back
movement in Black

**III.**

I am the Black woman

I am Bessie Smith
singing the blues
& all the Bessies
that never sang a note

I'm the southerner
who went north
I'm the northerner
who went down home

I'm the teacher
in the all-Black school

I'm the graduate
who cannot read

I'm the social worker
in the city ghetto
I'm the car hop
in a delta town

I'm the junkie with a jones
I'm the dyke in the bar
I'm the matron at a county jail
I'm the defendant with nothin' to say.

I'm the woman with 8 kids
I'm the woman who didn't have any
I'm the woman who's poor as sin
I'm the woman who's got plenty

I'm the woman who
raised white babies &
taught my kids to
raise themselves.

movement in Black
movement in Black
can't keep em back
movement in Black

**IV.**

Roll call, shout em out

Phillis Wheatley
Sojourner Truth
Harriet Tubman
Frances Ellen Watkins Harper
Stagecoach Mary

Lucy Prince
Mary Pleasant
Mary McLeod Bethune
Rosa Parks
Coretta King
Fannie Lou Hamer
Marian Anderson
& Billies
& Bessie
sweet Dinah
A-re-tha
Natalie
Shirley Chisholm
Barbara Jordan
Patricia Harris
Angela Davis
Flo Kennedy
Zora Neal Hurston
Nikki Giovanni
June Jordan
Audre Lorde
Edmonia Lewis
and me
and me
and me
and me
and me
& all the names we forgot to say
& all the names we didn't know
& all the names we don't know, yet.

movement in Black
movement in Black
Can't keep em back
movement in Black

## V.

I am the Black woman
I am the child of the sun
the daughter of dark
I carry fire to burn the world
I am water to quench its throat
I am the product of slaves
I am the offspring of queens
I am still as silence
I flow as the stream

I am the Black woman
I am a survivor
I am a survivor
I am a survivor
I am a survivor
I am a survivor

Movement in Black.

# BEING GAY

Move in darkness
know the touch of a woman


a wall of normalcy
wraps your body –
strangles
brightens

wrinkled ugliness

sin

fear

admissions


Two days later

you shudder

& take 2 aspirins

**1.**

My lover is a woman
  & when i hold her –
    feel her warmth –
    i feel good – feel safe

then/ i never think of
  my families' voices –
  never hear my sisters say –
  bulldaggers, queers, funny –
  come see us, but don't
  bring your friends –
  it's okay with us,
  but don't tell mama
    it'd break her heart
  never feel my father
  turn in his grave
  never hear my mother cry
  Lord, what kind of child is this?

**2.**

My lover's hair is blonde
  & when it rubs across my face
    it feels soft –
  feels like a thousand fingers
  touch my skin & hold me
  and i feel good.

then/ i never think of the little boy
  who spat & called me a nigger
  never think of the policemen
  who kicked my body and said crawl

never think of Black bodies
hanging in trees or filled
with bullet holes
never hear my sisters say
white folks hair stinks
don't trust any of them
never feel my father
turn in his grave
never hear my mother talk
of her backache after scrubbing floors
never hear her cry —
Lord, what kind of child is this?

**3.**

My lovers eyes are blue
& when she looks at me
i float in a warm lake
   feel my muscles go weak with want
      feel good — feel safe

Then/ i never think of the blue
   eyes that have glare at me —
   moved three stools away from me
     in a bar
   never hear my sisters rage
   of syphilitic Black men as
     guinea pigs —
   rage of sterilized children —
   watch them just stop in an
   intersection to scare *the old*
     *white bitch.*
   never feel my father turn
   in his grave
   never remember my mother
   teaching me the yes sirs & mams
     to keep me alive —

never hear my mother cry,
Lord, what kind of child is this?

**4.**

And when we go to a gay bar
    & my people shun me because i crossed
       the line
    & her people look to see what's
    wrong with her – what defect
    drove her to me –

And when we walk the streets
    of this city – forget and touch
    or hold hands and the people
    stare, glare, frown, & taunt
    at those queers –

I remember –
    Every word taught to me
    Every word said to me
    Every deed done to me
    & then i hate –
    i look at my lover
    & for an instant – doubt –

Then/ i hold her hand tighter
And i can hear my mother cry.
Lord, what kind of child is this.

# Cop-out
## (To My Mother)

"i like your friends.
they're real people.
not phony – like your
sisters' friends."

Marie Cooks

All of these
real people –
are real,
  live in the
    flesh
      dykes –
& all the boyfriends
  that they have
  are a part of my creativity.

All of these real people
  are real –
& i can only tell you
  real live in the flesh –
    lies –

# For Willyce

When i make love to you
    i try
        with each stroke of my tongue
           to say    i love you
           to tease           i love you
           to hammer    i love you
           to melt   i love you

    & your sounds drift down
        oh god!
           oh jesus!
    and i think –
here it is, some dude's
getting credit for what
        a woman
        has done,
          again.

# Best Friends
## (for Whitey)

So how come
we can't touch
when we hurt most?
        Can only
        sense &
        hurl ourselves
against forces
& each other
& laugh away
our agony
        tomorrow –
as drunk
yesterdays.

# Pit Stop

A pit is a covered hole
used to trap wild animals.

a pit is an abyss.

a pit is the ground floor
of a theater,
especially the part
at the rear.

a pit is a coward's suicide.

a hearty drink to anything –

Let us drink to your new lover
Let us drink to your lover – gone
Let us drink to my lover
Let us drink to my lover – gone
Hey let's drink to the good people
Let's drink to the nearest holiday

Let's drink to our ability to drink.

A pit is a covered hole

used by wild animals.

it's hard to withdraw the fangs, now

in public places

the anger spills over

to be mopped away, later

too much drink

slow fang withdrawal

our animalism is showing

a bad image –

Let's drink to a bad image

Let's drink to a covered pit

  & happy animals

& withdrawn fangs.

a pit is an abyss.

Let's drink to my shame

    a hustle

a grand hustle

i love you, so

i won't call you fool

Let's have another drink

you love me

you won't walk away from me.

Let's have another drink

    to our hustle

let's hustle another drink

    & drink

to our ability to hustle.

Let's have a drink to our shame.

Let's have a drink

    to drink

a pit is the ground floor

of a theater,

especially the part

at the rear.

It was a good show last night

full of venom

i thought for sure she would hit her

& did you see that woman fall off her stool?

yes indeed a grand show

everybody was

& it ended safely –

How's your head this morning dearie?

Let's drink to a good show

Let's drink to the rear of the theater.

It's hard to get hit with a bottle here.

Just to watch the show.

Let's drink to a ground floor.

Has anyone ever priced the
                balcony?

a pit is a coward's suicide.

what do you mean kill yourself?

that's a bummer – makes me sad.

Let's have another drink.

yes, i've gained weight –
it's the beer you know.

cold – yes
caught a lot of colds –

just need to take more vitamin C

Let's have a hot toddy for my cold.

Wow that's too bad – overdose huh

won't touch the stuff –

*if*    anything kills me
it will be the booze, ha ha.

Let's have a drink to her & her drug

she was a good kid

One of these days i'll have a check-up

getting winded too easily – getting old.

Let's have another drink.

i can't imagine anyone committing suicide.

the mechanics are too slow here.

the tires should be on –
     the gas in.

what's the matter?

you want to cost us the race?


Oh – one more drink

Let's drink to the race.
let's drink to the pit crew.
Let's drink,
     let's drink
let us drink
     let us drink
          drink
               drink

excuse me friends,
     i must go now

i cannot afford to lose
     this race.

i cannot afford to die,
     in this place

*Give strong drink unto him that is ready to*
*perish, and wine unto those that be of*
*heavy hearts. Let him drink and forget his*
*poverty, and remember his misery no more.*
Proverbs 31: 6-7

When i drink
    i scream
    i fight
    i cry

    i don't
     do these things

      when i'm sober

so far,

my friends

think the
solution

to my being

a problem

is for me
to stop

drinking.

# For the Straight Folks
# Who Don't Mind Gays
# But Wish They Weren't So BLATANT

you know some people
got a lot of nerve.
sometimes, i don't believe
the things i see and hear.

Have you met the woman
who's shocked by 2 women kissing
& in the same breath,
tells you that she's pregnant?
BUT GAYS SHOULDN'T BE BLATANT.

Or this straight couple
sits next to you in a movie
& you can't hear the dialogue
Cause of the sound effects.
BUT GAYS SHOULDN'T BE BLATANT.

And the woman in your office
Spends the entire lunch hour
talking about her new bikini drawers
& how much her husband likes them.
BUT GAYS SHOULDN'T BE BLATANT.

Or the "hip" chick in your class,
rattling a mile a minute –
while you're trying to get stoned
in the john
about the camping trip she took
with her musician boyfriend.
BUT GAYS SHOULDN'T BE BLATANT.

You go in a public bathroom
and all over the walls
there's John loves Mary,
Janice digs Richard,
Pepe loves Delores, etc. etc.
BUT GAYS SHOULDN'T BE BLATANT.

Or you go to an amusement park
& there's a tunnel of love
& pictures of straights
painted on the front
& grinning couples
coming in and out.
BUT GAYS SHOULDN'T BE BLATANT.

Fact is, blatant heterosexuals
are all over the place.
Supermarkets, movies, on your job,
in church, in books, on television
every day and night, every place –
even in gay bars.
& they want gay men & women
to go hide in the closets –

So to you straight folks
i say – Sure, i'll go
if you go too,
but i'm polite
so – after you.

# My Lady Ain't No Lady

my lady ain't no lady

she doesn't flow into a room –
she enters & her presence is felt.
she doesn't sit small –
she takes her space.
she doesn't partake of meals –
she eats – replenishes herself

my lady ain't no lady –

she has been known
     to speak in a loud voice,
     to pick her nose,
     stumble on a sidewalk,
     swear at her cats,
     swear at me,
     scream obscenities at men,
     paint rooms,
     repair houses,
     tote garbage,
     play basketball,
     & numerous other
     un ladylike things.

my lady is definitely no lady
which is fine with me,

cause i ain't no gentleman.

# Non-monogamy
# Is A Pain in the Butt

I have a lover
who has a lover
who has a lover
now, ain't that hot.

So one day
i say, hey
why don't you stay?
she said, tonight
i'd rather not.

My lover and me
decided to be
two, not four or three
surely you see,
but thanks a lot.

I have a lover
who has a lover
who has a lover
now that's a dumb spot.

But it's okay
tomorrow we'll play
be loving and gay
maybe stroll by the bay
& take pictures of yachts.

So don't laugh, he hee
at my lovers and me
what a strange place to be
For you can't foresee
what's to be your lot.

Maybe one day
*you* will say

with hair turning gray
and heart heavy as clay
lying alone on a cot.

I have a lover
who has a lover
who has a lover
now ain't that hot.

# LOVE POEMS

love

& friendship

are words of

people

telling

people

trust is
a word
for
bankers

me

& you

&
You

are

words

for

us.

Let me come to you naked
come without my masks
come dark
    and lay beside you

Let me come to you old
come as a dying snail
come weak
    and lay beside you

Let me come to you angry
come shaking with hate
come callused
    and lay beside you

even more

Let me come to you strong
come sure and free
come powerful

and lay with you.

I have a solitary lover
　she digs it
　　moves with it
　　　moves
　　　　alone well
　　　moves alone
　　　　　　　well
i have a solitary
　　　lover
she digs it
she digs moving
　digs
　　moving
　alone
& when i barge
　into her world
　　she
　　　in spite of herself
　　graciously
　　　　　　comes
　　with me
　　　　　calms with me
　　　solitary

# I Kumquat You

Some one said

    to say

I love you –

    is corny.

# A Small Contradiction

It is politically incorrect
   to demand monogamous
      relationships –

It's emotionally insecure
   to seek
      ownership of
   another's soul
               or body     &
damaging to one's psyche
to restrict the giving and
      taking of love.

   Me, i am
totally opposed to
monogamous relationships
      unless
         I'm
      in love.

i wish that i could hate you
when you brush against me in sleep
your breath slapping life in my innards
& i feel my body go soft in wanting you
i wish right then that i could hate you

i wish that i could hate you
when i sit not able to see you
cursing the something that came up
& know i will still come when you call –
i wish right then that i could hate you

i wish that i could hate you
when i hear you on the phone
planning time away from me
& wish it was me that you're talking to
i wish right then i could hate you

I wish for enough anger to hate you
– My love for you keeps getting in my way.

Bitch!
i want to scream
I hate you
Fuck you for this pain
You used my guts
& now you stand here
Write my pain off
an unworkable experience
Bitch!
i want to scream –
& the words –
– unreal
from my mouth
i love you –
i hope you'll be happy.

Sitting here,
      listening to you
make music.
      i realized
the many years
      we
                  have known each other
      is
one month.

      so instead
                  of running upstairs
& sticking my tongue
      in your ear
                  i'll give you
                              this.

Both gestures
      mean
            the same.

Woman, i love you.

If it were possible
to place you in my brain,
to let you roam
around in and out
my thought waves –
you would never
have to ask –
why do you love me?

This morning as you slept,
I wanted to kiss you awake –
say "i love you" til your brain
smiled and nodded "yes"
this woman does love me.

Each day the list grows –
filled with the things that are you
things that make my heart jump –
Yet, words would sound strange;
become corny in utterance.

Now, each morning when i wake
i don't look out my window
to see if the sun is shining –
I turn to you – instead.

# I Have

i have known
many women
& the you of you
     puzzles me.

it is not beauty
     i have known
beautiful women.

it is not brains
     i have known
intelligent women.

it its not goodness
     i have known
good women.

it is not selflessness
     i have known
giving women.

Yet, you touch me
     in new,
       different
         ways

i become sand
on a beach
washed anew with
each wave of you.

with each touch of you
i am fresh bread
warm and rising

i become a new-born kitten
ready to be licked
& nuzzled into life.

You are my last love
And my first love
You make me a virgin –

& I want to give myself to you

# On Jealousy

it's insane
& childish
you say
your feelings –
make you embarrassed

my body responds to you –
glows with your touch
feels mellow –
safe & protected.
childish,
insane, you say –

no say i –
i worry about
people who don't
care for
or value
their
possessions

As you entered
        my life –
it was so easy
        to accept –
for years
i have
visualized
you & me
        on beaches
        in stores
        at movies
        in bed

Fantasy is the food
            of poets
what blew my mind –
is when i pinched
myself to wake up –
        & YOU
were still
        here.

# Metamorphosis

you take these fingers
    bid them soft –
a velvet touch
    to your loins

you take these arms
    bid them pliant
a warm cocoon
    to shield you

you take this shell
    bid it full
a sensual cup
    to lay with you

you take this voice
    bid it sing
an uncaged bird
    to warble your praise

you take me, love
    a sea skeleton
fill me with you
    & i become
pregnant with love
    give birth
        to revolution

# Para Maria Sandra

Pain, like fertilizer
can be used for growth
can be worked
deep inside –
nurtured
turned to blossoms.

I have felt you
pequena gigante
as I move
across the land
of your past

Seen the strength
of your reds & browns
– the subtle power.

To ease your pain
to soothe your anger
i would become
the grandmother
would stroke your hair
and lie
es nada, niña
es nada.

I would become
the unknown father
would take you
in my arms
& speak to you
of my pride
sing praise of
our blood.

I would become
the brother
locked in silence –
trapped in manhood
would speak
forever of love
be gentle & touch

To ease your pain
i would become
a chameleon
change to your needs
i would become
tu familia
te amo
pequena gigante
te amo.

# gente

It's difficult to explain
a good feeling –
my world has become colorful –
a rainbow of hues
now – a part of my living
        and it feels good.

it feels good
to listen to people
talk about the streets
& know
it's not a *vicarious* experience.

it feels good
to sit and be loose
to talk, without worry,
about the racist in the room.

it feels good
to hear
'we're gonna have a party'
& know it's really
going to be party.

it feels good
to be able to say
my sisters
and not have
*any* reservations.

But best of all –
it feels good
to sit in a room
and say
'Have you ever felt like...?'
and somebody has.

# Group

*"The primary lesson learned by any
minority is self-hatred."*

I do not know
when my lessons began

I have no memory –
        of a teacher,
        or books.

osmosis – perhaps
the lessons slip
into my brain
my cells – silently

I do have memory of
childhood chants

if you're white – alright
if you're brown – stick around
if you're Black – get back

I do have memory of teachers

*"you are heathens
why can't you be
like the white kids
you are bad – "*

        Bad

& I never thought
to ask the Black teachers
in the all-Black schools
how did they know
how white kids were?

Bad

I do have memory
of playground shouts
*"your lips are too big"*
a memory of my sisters
putting on lipstick
on half of their lips
to make them look smaller

Bad

*"your hair nappy"*
I do have memory
of "Beauty" parlours
& hot combs and grease

Bad

*"stay out of the sun*
*it'll make you darker"*
I do have memory
of Black & White
bleaching cream
Nadinola
Bleach & Glow

Bad

*"your nose is too big"*
I do have memory
of mothers pinching
their babies' noses
to make them smaller
        Bad
        BAD
I do not know
when my lessons

began
do not know
when my lessons
        were learned,
absorbed into my cells

        now
there are new lessons
        new teachers
each week I go to my group
        see women
                        Black women
Beautiful Black Women
& I am in love
                        with each of them
& this is important
        in the loving
in the act of loving
        each woman
I have learned a new lesson
I have learned
        to love myself

# The Law

In my youth
i was taught
the law is good –
my parents,
my teachers,
    all
told of policemen
to help me find my way –
of courts, to punish
those who would harm me
i was taught
"respect the law"
Now, in my third decade
I have seen the law

the law
comes to homes
& takes the poor
for traffic tickets
the law
takes people to jail
for stealing food
the law
comes in mini-skirts
to see if your home
is bare enough
for welfare
the law
sits in robes
in courtrooms
& takes away
your children
the law
arrests the prostitute
but not her customer

the law
sends a rich woman
to jail on weekends
for murder
sends a porno bookseller
to jail for 30 years
the law
tries women who kill
rapists &
frees the rapist
because rape
is a "normal"
reaction
And my mind reels
    contradictions
    contra/
        dictions
& the voices from
my youth declare

the law is *good*
the law is *fair*
the law is *just*
& then I realize
good, fair, just,
are all 4 letter words
& to use 4 letter words
is against the law

# WOMAN SLAUGHTER

# PAT PARKER

# Womanslaughter

It doesn't hurt as much now –
the thought of you dead
doesn't rip at my innards,
leaves no holes to suck rage.
Now, thoughts of the four
daughters of Buster Cooks,
children, survivors
of Texas Hell, survivors
of soul-searing poverty,
survivors of small town
mentality, survivors
now three
doesn't hurt as much.

I.

An Act

I used to be fearful
of phone calls in the night –
never in the day.

Death, like the vampire,
fears the sun
never in the day –
"Hello, Patty."
"Hey, big sister
what's happening?
How's the kids?"
"Patty, Jonesy shot Shirley,
She didn't make it."

Hello, Hello Death
Don't you know it's daytime?
The sun is much too bright today
Hello, Hello Death

you made a mistake
came here too soon, again.
Five months, Death
My sisters and I just met
in celebration of you –
We came, the four strong
daughters of Buster Cooks,
and buried him –
We came, the four strong
daughters of Buster Cooks,
and took care of his widow.
We came, the four strong
daughters of Buster Cooks
and shook hands with his friends.
We came, the four strong
daughters of Buster Cooks,
and the right flowers.
We came, the four strong
daughters of Buster Cooks,
walked tall & celebrated you.
We came, his four strong daughters,
and notified insurance companies
arranged social security payments
gathered the sum of his life.

"We must be strong for mother."

She was the third daughter of Buster Cooks.
I am the fourth.
And in his death we met.
The four years that separated us – gone.
And we talked.
She would divorce the quiet man.
Go back to school – begin again.
Together we would be strong
& take care of Buster's widow.
The poet returned to the family.
The fourth daughter came home.

Hello, Hello Death
What's this you say to me?
Now there are three.
We came, the three sisters
of Shirley Jones
& took care of her mother.
We picked the right flowers,
contacted insurance companies,
arranged social security payments,
and cremated her.
We came, the three sisters
of Shirley Jones.
We were not strong.
"It is good, they said,
that Buster is dead.
He would surely kill
the quiet man."

II.

Justice

There was a quiet man
He married a quiet wife
Together, they lived
a quiet life.

Not so, not so
her sisters said,
the truth comes out
as she lies dead.
He beat her.
He accused her
of awful things
& he beat her.
One day she left.

"Hell, Hello Police
I am a woman
& I am afraid
My husband means to kill me."

She went to her sister's house
she, too, was a woman alone.
The quiet man came & beat her.
Both women were afraid.

"Hello, Hello Police
I am a woman
& I am afraid.
My husband means to kill me."

The four strong daughters
of Buster Cooks
came to bury him —
the third one carried a gun.
"Why do you have a gun?"
"For protection — just in case."
"Can you shoot it?"
"Yes, I have learned well."

"Hello, Hello Police
I am a woman alone
& I am afraid.
My husband means to kill me."

"Lady, there's nothing we can do
until he tries to hurt you.
Go to the judge & he will decree
that your husband leaves you be."
She found an apartment
with a friend.
She would begin
a new life again.

Interlocutory Divorce Decree in hand;
The end of the quiet man.
He came to her home
& he beat her.
Both women were afraid.

"Hello, Hello Police
I am a woman alone
& I am afraid.
My ex-husband means to kill me."

"Fear not, lady,
he will be sought."
It was *too* late
when he was caught.
One day a quiet man
shot his quiet wife
three times in the back.
He shot her friend as well.
His wife died.

The three sisters
of Shirley Jones
came to cremate her.
They were not strong.

III.

Somebody's Trial

"It is good, they said,
that Buster is dead.
He would surely kill
the quiet man."
I was not at the trial.
I was not needed to testify.
She slept with other men, he said.

No, said her friends.
No, said her sisters.
That is a lie.
She was Black.
You are white.
Why were you there?
We were friends, she said.
I was helping her move
the furniture; the divorce court
had given it to her
Were you alone? they asked.
No two men came with us.
They were gone with a load.
She slept with women, he said.
No, said her sisters.
No, said her friends.
We were only friends.
That is a lie.
You lived with this woman?
Yes, said her friend.
You slept in the same bed?
Yes, said her friend.
Were you lovers?
No, said her friend.
But you slept in the same bed?
Yes, said her friend.

What shall be done with this man?
Is it a murder of the first degree?
No, said the men,
It is a crime of passion.
He was angry.

Is it a murder of the second degree?
Yes, said the men,
but we will not call it that.
We must think of his record.

We will call it manslaughter.
The sentence is the same.
What will we do with this man?
His boss, a white man came.
This is a quiet Black man, he said.
He works well for me
The men sent the quiet
Black man to jail.
He went to work in the day.
He went to jail & slept at night.
In one year, he went home.

**IV.**

Woman-slaughter

"It is good, they said,
that Buster is dead.
He would surely kill
the quiet man."

Sister, I do not understand.
I rage & do not understand.
In Texas, he would be freed.
One Black kills another
One less Black for Texas.
But this is not Texas.
This is California.
The city of angels.
Was his crime so slight?
George Jackson served
years for robbery.
Eldridge Cleaver served
years for rape.
I know of a man in Texas
who is serving 40 years
for possession of marijuana.
Was his crime so slight?

What was his crime?
He only killed his wife.
But a divorce I say.
Not final, they say;
Her things were his
including her life.
Men cannot rape their wives.
Men cannot kill their wives.
They passion them to death.

The three sisters
of Shirley Jones
came & cremated her
& they were not strong.
Hear me now –
it is almost three years
& I am again strong.

I have gained many sisters.
And if one is beaten,
or raped, or killed,
I will not come in mourning black.
I will not pick the right flowers.
I will not celebrate her death
& it will matter not
if she's Black or white –
if she loves women or men.
I will come with my many sisters
and decorate the streets
with the innards of those
brothers in womenslaughter.
No more, can I dull my rage
in alcohol & deference
to *men's* courts.
I will come to my sisters,
not dutiful,
I will come strong.

# Autumn Morning
## (for Shirley)

Tree –
    that lives
    & feeds
    & feels
–from the living
–from the dead
      you grow.

Tree –
    in time,
i will move
in dawn stillness,
    with you.

*Her children arise up, and call her blessed...*
                    Proverbs 31:28

when i was a child
i was punished –
i refused to say
yes sir & yes mam.
i was – they said
disrespectful –
should extend
        courtesy –
defer to age.
i believe
respect
is earned –
does not come
with birth.
now, my mother
is dying
& i wish to say
so much
to thank her
to say – i love you
to hold her in my arms.
these things
i cannot do/
we have too
many years
of not touching –
of not saying
instead – i sit
& watch her sleep –
see her breathe –

labor
cringe at the tubes
in her body/
watch the strength
    seep away
i am afraid of death
fear to touch a cold body
yet, i know
in the final viewing,
i will lean over my mother
& whisper in her ear —
yes mam, mama, yes mam.

there is a woman in this town

she goes to different bars
sits in the remotest place
watches the other people
drinks till 2 & goes home – alone

some say she is lonely
some say she is an agent
none of us speak to her

Is she our sister?

there is a woman in this town
she lives with her husband
she raises her children
she says she is happy
& is not a women's libber

some say she is mis-guided
some say she is an enemy
none of us know her

Is she our sister?

there is a women in this town

she carries a lot of weight
her flesh triples on her frame
she comes to all the dances
dances a lot; goes home – alone

some say she's a lot of fun
some say she is too fat
none of us have loved her

Is she our sister?

there is a woman in this town

she owns her own business
she goes to work in the day
she goes home at night
she does not come to the dances

some say she is a capitalist
some say she has no consciousness
none of us trust her

Is she our sister?

there is a woman in this town

she comes to all the parties
wears the latest men's fashions
calls the women mama
& invites them to her home

some say she's into roles
some say she hates herself
none of us of us go out with her

Is she our sister?

there is a woman in this town

she was locked up
she comes to many meetings
she volunteers for everything
she cries when she gets upset

some say she makes them nervous
some say she's too pushy
none of us invite her home

Is she our sister?

there is a woman in this town

she fills her veins with dope
goes from house to house to sleep
borrows money wherever she can
she pays it back if she must

some say she is a thief
some say she drains their energy
none of us have trusted her

Is she our sister?

      once upon a time, there was a dream
a dream of women. a dream of women
coming together and turning the world
around. turning the world around and making it over
a dream of women, all women being sisters.
a dream of caring; a dream of protection, a dream
of peace.

once upon a time, there was a dream
a dream of women. for the women who rejected the
dream; there had only been a reassurance. for the
women who believed the dream – there is dying, women,
sisters dying
      once upon a time there was a dream, a dream of women
turning the world all over, and it still lives –
it lives for those who would be sisters.

it lives for those who need a sister
it lives for those who once upon a time had a dream.

# NEW WORK

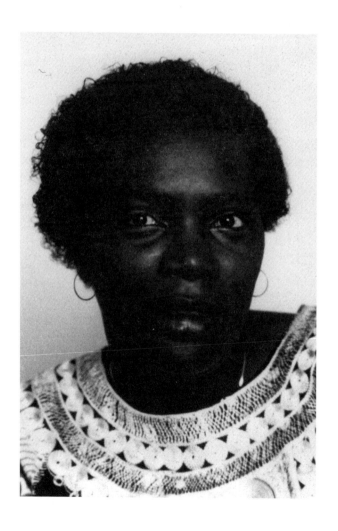

# Great God

I saw God today.
He wore a Van Heusen shirt
with a Brooks Brothers suit
Stacy Adams shoes
& a Stetson hat.

I saw God today.
He drove a white Lincoln
with red upholstery
power steering, safety belts
& a torn Goldwater sticker.

I saw God today.
He stopped at the drugstore
bought *Time* magazine
got a shoeshine
tipped the boy a dime.

I saw God today.
He read about Vietnam
took his family to see *Mary Poppins*
bought 3 popcorns, 2 grapes & a lime.

I saw God today.
He played a round of golf
told a nigger joke in the clubhouse
gave his maid the day off –
to get married.

# Between the Light

all
the sounds
     moving
           swinging
               past
me
and you
     moving
           swinging
               drift
in/out
fear not little children
sounds
beating a fast temp
and you
and i
     caught
           dancing
               between the light

# Sublimation

It has been said that
sleep is a short death.

I watch you, still,
your breath moving –
soft summer breeze.

Your face velvet
the tension of our love,
gone.

No, false death is not here
in our bed
just you – asleep
& me – wanting
to make love to you

writing words instead.

# Massage
## (for Margaret)

In the days following my mastectomy
my body was covered in bandages
mountains of tape hid the space
where my breast had been,
piled so high
the breast was still there.

My body numb
hard like my mother's body
in her casket
and I mourned
mourned for the passion gone
and I numbed my mind

No one had seen my body
except for my lover and my surgeon.
I protected my friends from robes,
my gymmates with towels

protected myself
no looks of horror
     pity
             disgust
Let the numbness be still.

I had a massage appointment
and I brought my numb self
turned my body into bread
for your hands to knead and mold
to stroke the tension
away
     away
          away

Like the fine bread I rise
my body loose and smoother
     tensing
            passionate
and I want to sing
I reawake
I want to kiss you
instead I say thank you
and go home.

# Reputation

Has anyone ever wondered
as I wonder
why
Fred Astaire
is hailed as the greatest
dancer in cinema HIStory?

I've watched him
spin, twirl, even tap
across the screen
with Ginger Rogers

And each time I see them
do the same dance
dance the same steps
I can't help but notice
she's the one
doing it
in high heels.

# Progeny

Three young Black women
descendants of three dead Black men
sit in a row
on a syndicated tv show.

Medgar, Martin, and Malcolm
their progeny tells of
growing up orphaned
by assassins' fury.

One tired white man
bold enough to ask
he proudly states
what others think
in silence.

"Why are we still
bringing this stuff up?
Black folks are doing fine, now."

| Eleanor Bumpurs | 66 | Black | dead |
| Clifford Glover | 10 | Black | dead |
| Allene Richardson | 64 | Black | dead |
| Randy Evans | 15 | Black | dead |

They are all dead
and doing fine, now.

I listen as Ms. Evers
tells how her father
taught his children to
drop to the floor
and crawl at the sound
of any loud noise
crawl away from danger.

She crawled that night
in Mississippi
her father on
their front porch dying
as she crawled.

And I think of my daughter
my beautiful child
who will never know
the sense of exploring
on a walk to school
because I am too fearful.

Is it time to teach her?
Must she learn to crawl?

I remember the lessons
 *say ma'am and sir*
 *cast your eyes down*
 *don't show your feeling*
 *be home before dusk.*

The voice of Ms. King
brings me back as
she says no, I
have not recovered
I will never recover
but I had my mother
and she was strong.

Those strong mothers.

Media images fill my vision
 weeping women, quiet women
  stunned women, angry women
dressed in funeral black
trailing flower-heavy coffins
with their babies in them.

Emmett Till's mother was strong.
Bobby Hutton's mother was strong.
Jonathan Jackson's mother was strong.

In the 1980s
in modern day amerika
young Black men have a
1 in 200 hundred chance
of being killed before
the age of twenty-five.

All the strong mothers-to-be
who will trail those coffins.

And I think of my child
my beautiful child
and I am fearful.
        Will she trail my coffin?
        Will I trail hers?

I hear  Ms. Shabazz say
my father was a gentle man
he taught us love
and to respect all mankind.

And I think of my child
my beautiful child
she smiles and laughs
she is fearful of no one.
        Is it time now
        for her lessons?
I must teach her
to be open
with reservations
to be bold
but caution
to love
and be wary.

I must teach her
to know her past
and not hate
in her present.

She must learn the lessons
of my mother and
her mother before her

and yet I want her to learn
new lessons
lessons not taught to me.

Is it difficult
to teach my child
the beauty of flowers
in a field
at the same time
I warn her about
the dangers of
open spaces.

# It's Not So Bad

It's not so bad
when your life is
enclosed in parentheses
    born
     died
definite and final.

It's not so bad
when the unknown
becomes known
   cause of death
     time

are projected on
scales and graphs
like tide flows.

It's not so bad
when friends ask
how are you? and
you see their bodies
   tensed
     buffered
for your answer.

It's not so bad
as the distance
   lengthens
     clear walls build
between you and
the healthy ones.

What really hurts
causes heartache
and silent screams

is to watch people
   prepare
      for your death
and you haven't.

# For Audre

*I.*

> *The Black Unicorn is restless*
> *The Black Unicorn is unrelenting*
> *The Black Unicorn is not free.*
> The Black Unicorn

Who is this bitch?
I mean really
  who is this bitch?

She come bopping
into my life

BOLD!

I be sitting in my pad
minding my own business
she come waltzing in
a funnel of energy
fire questions at me
like some *60 Minutes*
reporter hot
and the bad guy.

        Like where is she from?

I know literally
how she got here.

Been hanging around
with East Bay dykes
and wants to know
where the Black women are
    and
      to them I am
        the Black women.

Now this woman
sits in my house
reads
  no devours
     my words.

No comment.

Just
clicking and um-humming
then has the nerve
to say
I write good but
not enough.

*Push more*
*take the harder road.*

I know her for all
of an hour and a half
and she's talking at me
like my fifth grade teacher.

*More discipline, Patricia.*

*Stretch yourself.*

I mean really!
this be one bold-ass bitch.

If that's not enough
she ends the visit
  if that's what you call it

      I'd call it an earthquake
      shake everything that isn't
      nailed down loose
      watch it crumble and fall

she tells me to my face
as she goes out my door
"you need to get rid of
your lover –
she no help to you."

Who is this bitch?

II.

> *I am*
> *woman*
> *and not white.*
> A Woman Speaks

You talk to me
like my mother
with your eyes

dark pieces of coal
pierce my words
dare me to be
untruthful

reach beneath the surface
tell you the part
that I hold back.

I have known you forever
been aware that you would come.

My muse sang of you –
        watch the sky for
        an ebony meteorite
        that will pierce
        into the darkness
        illuminate your fears

hurl them at you
laughing.

*Are you quick
enough to survive?*

*Can I count on you
to be there?*

**III.**

> *I am often afraid to this day, but even more so angry at having to
> be afraid, of having to spend so much of my energies, interrupting
> my work, simply upon fear and worry.*
>             The Cancer Journals

After I read *The Cancer Journals*
I made love to you

touched your body – pressed
my hands deep into your flesh
and passed my warmth to you.

I kissed the space where
your right breast had been
ran my tongue over your body
        to lick away your fear
        to lick away my fear.

I felt jealous
wanted to be near you
and to hold you
and to sing you songs
        to say I love you
        you are not alone
then
I felt guilt
        for all the unsent letters

for all the unwritten poems
for all the "dead air."

**IV.**

*Every woman I have ever loved has left her print upon me.*
Zami: A New Spelling of My Name

"I was ready to give you up"
so much time passed
and no sense of you.

Sister, love
some things are not possible.
I carry you with me
talk with you
ask your opinion

you cannot give me up
I cannot give you up.

We are linked
        in
            our Blackness
            our creativity
            our queerness
our muses conspire.

I never promise
        to write often
        to call often
        to be a presence

I promise
        to call you
        and call you
        sister.

# Funny

Once upon a time there was a young woman. Her name was Doris, or Sarah, or Sue; I never knew. She walked the streets of Sunnyside, the beaten seashells dusted her feet and she always walked alone. She wore men's clothing, long before profiteers had developed unisex wear: flannel shirts in fall, covered by an army field jacket in the winter; white T-shirts in summer, and khaki pants. Not blue jeans, which were acceptable for young women after school and on Saturdays, but beige khaki pants. Men's pants.

Every evening around dusk she walked the three blocks from her house to Mr. Isom's store. She passed my house with long strides, her arms swinging; a steady rhythm, not too slow, not too fast. Her eyes were always forward. She never turned to the people sitting on their porches, never nodded her head, never said, "How you do?" She always walked straight and purposefully, and she always walked alone.

One day I asked my parents who she was, and they closed around me. My mother, who had taught me to always be nice ("if you can't say something good about a person, then say nothing at all") looked embarrassed and told, "You stay away from her – she's funny." I didn't understand. Had never heard anyone called funny except on radio and television as we crowded around the small screen, or box, and watched Amos and Andy, or George Burns and Gracie Allen, or listened to Fibber McGee and Molly.

"What do you mean, *funny?*"

I should have known better. I had lived with my parents long enough to recognize "the look." The look that said a subject was closed – no discussion here. You're too young, or innocent, or female, or Black to learn about this.

"Never you mind, girl. You jist do like your mama say and stay away from her. She's a disgrace. If I had a daughter like that, I'd kill her."

My father was not embarrassed. He was angry. The look that he wore when he came home at night. The look he wore when he had to change his plans cause Mr. Jenkins from the Oldsmobile place called and wanted to come retread his tires the very next day, not two days later. The look he wore when he had to wait for an hour to get paid while Mr. Jenkins waited on his customers, even though Daddy was done and needed to get to Mr. James's Buick place to retread tires that he also had to have done that same day.

I had seen that look, but I had never seen it directed toward a Black person who had said nothing, done nothing to my father and what was his.

So, I didn't find out what *funny* meant that day, and I never asked that woman her name or why she always walked alone.

The Fuqua family moved next door to us the year I was seven. There were four children: Joyce, Barbara, Howard, and Anthony, in that order. Joyce was four months younger than me.

We became inseparable. We rode bikes, played jacks, football, and paper dolls. Paper dolls were our lives. During the summer we would cut out models from ads in the *Houston Chronicle.* We had to use summer models because they wore shorts or bathing suits. We pasted cardboard on their backs to make them sturdy. Then we'd draw clothes – hundreds of outfits, many copied from JCPenney catalogs, or just what we thought the well-dressed doll should have.

Each of us had complete families. A mother, a father, a boy, and a girl. All-American nuclear family, and white.

We played paper dolls for hours. If Joyce's siblings had been good, or her mother insisted, then they were allowed to play with us. More often, we played alone.

The game changed the summer I was fourteen. In the past, we would press the dolls' faces together for their goodbye-I'm-going-to-work kiss and continue to play. This time it was different. Joyce reached out as the dolls touched and pulled me to her and kissed me. To this day I'm not sure why. Perhaps it was the sexual playing we had begun with the boys in the neighborhood, allowing them to sneak kisses and fast feels during hide-and-seek. Perhaps it was simply the time, as puberty took control of our loins and senses. Perhaps it was Joyce acting out what she had been secretly learning at Mr. Isom's store from Mrs. Isom. I don't know why, but we kissed.

From that moment, the games changed. We played paper dolls as often as we could, and we played alone. We never admitted that what we were doing had nothing to do with the paper dolls. We always took them out and dressed them; then we laid them down and took each other.

We kissed long, slow, passionate kisses, mounted each other rubbing our genitalia against one another, feeling our budding breasts.

Our parents marveled at how wonderfully we got along. We never fought; we cried when we couldn't spend the night at the other's house. Yes, we played paper dolls at night, too.

The summer I turned sixteen was the most exciting summer of my life. All my sisters had gone off to college and both my parents worked. That meant our house was mine and Joyce's. We spent hours each day exploring each other's bodies – until the day my father came home early.

I don't know how long my father had been standing there. As Joyce and I pulled apart to say goodbye, I saw him and I died. My heart stopped, my breathing stopped. I was numb. I knew in that instant that my life was over. I wasn't going to California that next year. I wasn't going to college. I was never going to see my mother or sisters again. I was never going to ride my bike or wrestle with my dog. I was going to die by my father's hand.

He didn't hit me. He told Joyce to go home, and then he turned and walked away. Joyce left immediately. She left her dolls, and left me to face the wrath of my father.

My father, who was known throughout my entire life as crazy, the man who insisted that all boyfriends come to our house and meet him, come pass his test of approval – and no boy ever passed – the man said not one word to me.

My mother came home and the two of them went into their bedroom and talked. Not for long, not more than two minutes. Then they came out. My mother cooked dinner, and I went into my room and prayed. I prayed that it was all a bad dream and I would wake up quickly. I prayed that my father would have a heart attack and die. I prayed that time would suspend itself and I would never have to deal with the next moment.

We ate dinner in complete silence that night. Not one word was said by anyone. I ate trying to pace my meal. I did not want to finish ahead of my folks – no way did I want to ask permission to leave the table. I wanted invisibility. I don't know what I ate, I only know it was heavy. Tons of rocks being passed down my throat. After dinner I went to bed and lay there, still praying: my father had that look, and my mother was worried.

My mother came into my room the next morning and told me to get dressed. To put on one of my school dresses. I asked no questions. School dress on a Saturday? You got it, Mom. We climbed into my father's car and drove to Third Ward. My curiosity was being squashed by fear. And my parents said nothing.

They took me to a doctor's office. I waited outside as they went into an exam room. A few minutes later I was called inside. My father left and my mother watched as this physician had me disrobe and looked at my breasts – not touching, just looking.

Then he had me lie down and looked at my genitals. Again not touching, just looking. I was told to get dressed and wait outside. My father re-entered the exam room. Less than ten minutes later we were out of the doctor's office and back in the car and headed home.

Still no one had said anything to me.

When we got home, my parents told me to go into the living room and sit down. They walked in together, and finally someone spoke to me. My father.

"The doctor says you are alright. You're not funny, so I don't ever expect you to do what I saw you and Joyce doing again."

They left the room. That was it. I was still alive, and now I knew what funny was.

The following day, after morning church service, my father took me to all of our neighbors' houses. I had to sit while he told each neighbor what he had caught Joyce and me doing. I didn't understand then that he was employing their aid in watching the two of us while he was at work. I thought the man had lost his mind and simply wanted to see me die from humiliation. Yet it didn't make sense because he had already told me I was alright – not funny.

Joyce and I still saw each other, still explored each other. We continued to do so until I left for college.

We didn't know the name for what we were and what we were doing, but we did know it had to be a secret. We had received our first closet keys. But faith, or time, or the goddess placed us in an era where closet doors would at first creak, then slide, then blast open. And unlike Doris, or Sarah, or Sue, or whatever her name was, we would not have to walk alone.

# Jonestown
# & Other Madness

JONESTOWN &
other madness

poetry by pat parker

# foreword

This book came about because we have become too quiet. We go to our jobs and raise our families and turn our minds away from the madness that surrounds us.

The tragedy of Jonestown occurred in 1978. It is amazing to me that we have not demanded better explanations of what happened. As I travel and talk with people, I find that most of them do not believe what they have been told. Yet we still know very little. I must ask the question: If 900 white people had gone to a country with a Black minister and 'committed suicide,' would we have accepted the answers we were given so easily?

I find it difficult to accept the answers of Jonestown. I find it equally difficult in the case of Priscilla Jones, or to realize that in 1984, straight people remain sufficiently terrified by the gay lifestyle that a gay rights bill protecting against job discrimination needs to be 'studied' by the governor of California.

Most of all, it is frightening to me that we live with the madness, that we continue to move through our lives as if these—and more—were normal occurrences. We are a nation in great trouble. It is time for those with vision to speak out loudly before the madness consumes us all.

Pat Parker
March 10, 1984
Oakland, California

# love isn't

I wish I could be
the lover you want
come joyful
bear brightness
like summer sun

Instead
I come cloudy
bring pregnant women
with no money
bring angry comrades
with no shelter

I wish I could take you
run over beaches
lay you in sand
and make love to you

Instead
I come rage
bring city streets
with wine and blood
bring cops and guns
with dead bodies and prison

I wish I could take you
travel to new lives
kiss ninos on tourist buses
sip tequila at sunrise

Instead
I come sad
bring lesbians
without lovers
bring sick folk
without doctors

bring children
without families

I wish I could be
your warmth
your blanket

All I can give
is my love.

I care for you
I care for our world
if I stop
caring about one
it would be only
a matter of time
before I stop
loving
the other.

# bar conversation

Three women were arrested for
assault recently after they beat
up a woman who put a swastika
on another woman's shoulder during
a S & M encounter

It's something you should write about.
If you talk about it
then women will listen
and know it's ok.
Now, envision one poet sitting in a bar
not cruising
observing the interactions
and then sitting face to face
with a young woman
who wants a spokesperson for
sado-masochism
among lesbians.
The first impulse is to dismiss
the entire conversation as more
ramblings of a *SWG*

    (read Silly White Girl:
    derogatory
    characterization
    used by minorities for
    certain members of the
    caucasian race.)

The second is to run rapidly
in another direction.
Polite poets do not run,
throw up, or strike
the other person in a conversation.
What we do is let our minds ramble.

So nodding in the appropriate places
I left the bar
traveled
first to the sixties
back to the cramped living rooms
activist dykes
consciousness-raising sessions
I polled the women there
one by one
Is this what it was all about?
Did we brave the wrath of threatened bar owners.
so women could wear handkerchiefs in their pockets?
one by one I asked.
Their faces faded
furrows of frowns on their brows
I went to the halls
where we sat hours upon hours
arguing with Gay men
trying to build a united movement
I polled the people there
one by one

Is this why we did it?
Did we grapple with our own who hated us
so women could use whips and chains?
The faces faded
puzzled faces drift out of vision.
I returned to the jails
where women sat bruised and beaten
singing songs of liberation
through puffed lips
I polled the women there
one by one
Is this why we did it?
Did we take to the streets
so women can carve swastikas on their bodies?

Hundreds and hundreds of women
pass by
no, march by
chant, sing, cry
I return to the voice
the young voice in the bar
and I am angry
the vision of women playing
as Nazis, policeman, rapists
taunts me
mocks me
words drift through

*it's always by consent*
*we are oppressed by other dykes*
*who don't understand*
and I am back in the bar
furious
the poll is complete
no, no no no
this is not why we did it
this is not why we continue to do.

We need not play at being victim
we need not practice pain
we need not encourage helplessness
they lurk outside of doors
follow us through the streets
and claim our lives daily.
We must not offer haven
for fascists and pigs
be it real or fantasy
the line is too unclear.

# my brother
## for Blackberri

I

It is a simple ritual.
Phone rings
Berri's voice
low, husky
'What's you're doing?'
'Not a thing,
you coming over?'
'Well, I thought I'd
come by."
A simple ritual.
He comes
we eat
watch television
play cards
play video games
some nights
he sleeps over
others
he goes home
sometimes
he brings a friend
more often
he doesn't.
A simple ritual.

II

It's a pause that alerts me
tells me this time
is hard time
the pain has risen
to the water line

we rarely verbalize
there is no need.

Within this lifestyle
there is much to undo you.

Hey look at the faggot!
When I was a child
our paper boy was Claude
every day
seven days a week
he bared the Texas weather
the rain that never stopped
walked through the Black section
where sidewalks had not
yet been invented
and ditches filled with water.
Walk careful Claude
across the plank
that serves as sidewalk
sometime tips into the murky water
or heat
wet heat
that covers your pores
cascades rivulets of
stinging sweat down your body.
Our paper boy Claude
bared the weather well
each day he came
and each Saturday at dusk
he would come to collect.

My parents liked Claude.
Each Saturday Claude polite
would come
always said thank you
whether we had the money

or not.
Each Saturday
my father would say
Claude is a nice boy
works hard
goes to church
gives money to his mother
and each Sunday
we would go to Church
and there would be Claude
in his choir robes
til the Sunday
when he didn't come.

Hey look at the faggot!

Some young men howled at him
ran in a pack
reverted to some ancient form
they took Claude
took his money
yelled faggot
as they cast his body
in front of a car.

III

How many cars have you dodged Berri?
How many ancient young men have you met?
Perhaps your size saved you
but then you were not always this size
perhaps your fleetness
perhaps
there are no more ancient young men.

Ah!   Within this lifestyle
we have chosen.

Sing?
What do you mean
you wanna be a singer?
Best get a good government job
maybe sing on the side.
You heard the words:
Be responsible
Be respectable
Be stable
Be secure
Be normal, boy.

How many quarter-filled rooms
have you sang your soul to
then washed away with
blended whiskey?

I told my booking agent one year
book me a tour
Blackberri and I
will travel this land
together
take our Black Queerness
into the face
of this place and say

Hey, here we are
a faggot & a dyke, Black
we make good music
& write good poems
We Be—Something Else.

My agent couldn't book us.
It seemed my lesbian audiences
were not ready for my faggot
brother
and I remembered

a law conference
in San Francisco
where women
women who loved women
threw boos and tomatoes
at a women who dared
to have a man in her band.

What is this world we have?
is my house the only safe place
for us?
And I am rage
all the low-paying gigs
all the uncut records
all the dodged cars
all the fear escaping
all the unclaimed love
so I could offer my bosom
and food
and shudder
fearful of the time
when it will not be
enough
fearful of the time
when the ritual
ends.

# georgia, georgia
# georgia on my mind

**I**

It came at first
like a rumor
traveling through
Black pages
of *Jet* and *Ebony*
children are missing
children are dead
in a southern metropolis
the common denominator
Black and young.

It comes again
now a nasty gnawing truth
Black bodies float up
from rivers and ditches
each week
more missing
more dead.

**II**

Now let the circus begin.
Proper politicians
come to town
reporters run from
family to family
look and see
the crying mother
at her child's funeral
look and see
the scared commissioners
'We're doing all we can.'

**III**

Fear raises its head
the unspoken belief
the killers
white,
the Klan, the Nazis
maniacs, crazies
genocide
eliminate the young
stop the breeding
Black friends angry
bitter scream
'those lousy bastards'
'those racist fiends'
white friends afraid
better to be quiet
and hope it's one insane fool.

**IV**

The lessons are
slowly slipped out
it's a shame *but*
if the kids were
not in the streets
Mother
why weren't you home
with your child?
the President says
he'll send more money for
investigation
two weeks after he
announced his budget cuts
the police psychologist
swears the killers
are Black

'the kids wouldn't trust
a white'
and half the nation prays
he's right.

My anger rises
I know who the killers are
and how the killer will go untried
see no court or judges
no jury or peers
the killers wear the suits of
businessmen
buy ghetto apartments
and overcharge the rent
the killers lock Black men
in prison or drive
them from their homes
the killers give the Black woman
a job
and pay her one-half of what she
needs to live
the killers scream about
juvenile crime
and refuse to build child-care centers.
it won't matter what
demented fool is caught
for society has provided
the lure.

A rich kid is not tempted
by candy
a rich kid is not tempted
by movies
a rich kid is not tempted
by attention.
Long after the murders of
Atlanta are solved
the killer will remain free.

# one thanksgiving day

One Thanksgiving Day
Priscilla Ford
got into her
Lincoln Continental
drove to Virginia Street
in downtown Reno
and ran over thirty people.
Six of them died.

One Thanksgiving Day
Priscilla Ford
got into her
Lincoln Continental
drove to Virginia Street
in downtown Reno
and ran over thirty people.
Six of them died.

Priscilla, Priscilla
who did you see?
what face from your past?
Was it the waitress
who waited to wait
on you?
Was it the clerk
who tried to sell you
only the
brightest colored clothes?
Was it your child's
teacher who tried to
teach her that she was
slow?
Was it the security guard
at the bank who guarded
you from the bank's money

with his eyes?
One Thanksgiving Day
Priscilla Ford
got into her
Lincoln Continental
drove to Virginia Street
in downtown Reno
and ran over thirty people.
Six of them died.

Screams filled the street
Panic ran through the crowd
like a losing streak
at the blackjack tables
and the state of Nevada
was stunned
A tired middle-aged Black woman
was not thankful that day
not thankful for her job
wrapping gifts at Macy's
not thankful for the state
taking custody of her child
she was not thankful
for her Lincoln Continental.

Priscilla Ford
got into her Lincoln Continental
and hurled through the streets of Reno
the killer made in Motown factories
swept down on tourists
looking to make a big hit
hit by a navy blue
steel bludgeon
screams dying beneath its wheels
and the state of Nevada
was angry.

She went to trial.
Insanity
her lawyers pled
she was crazy with anger
she was crazy with fear
she was crazy with defeat
she was crazy with isolation
no sane person kills
strangers with their cars
Priscilla Ford said yes
I drove my car
into the whiteness
of Nevada streets
she would say nothing more
and the state of Nevada
was frightened.
If Priscilla Ford could do it
who else?
How many Black faces
that emptied garbage
waited tables
bagged groceries
wrapped presents
were capable?

Reaction was swift.
One entrepreneur
printed a card
it said *Happy Thanksgiving*
with a picture of Priscilla
on its front
inside it said
*Sorry I Missed YOU.*

Priscilla Ford
got into her
Lincoln Continental

drove down Virginia Street
in downtown Reno
and ran over thirty people.
Six of them died
and the state of Nevada
was vindictive.
You cannot be insane
to be enraged is not insane
to be filled with hatred is not insane
to lash out at whiteness is not insane
it is being a nigger
it is your place in life.

Priscilla Ford
got into her
Lincoln Continental
drove to Virginia Street
in downtown Reno
and ran over thirty people.
Six of them died
and now Priscilla Ford
will die.
The state of Nevada
has judged

that it is
not crazy
for Black folks
to kill white folks
with their cars.

Priscilla Ford
will be
the second woman
executed in Nevada's history.
it's her highest
finish in life.

Photo from the papers of Pat Parker at The Arthur and Elizabeth Schlesinger Library on the History of Women in America, Radcliffe Institute for Advanced Study, Harvard University

207

# aftermath
## For Marty

Did you know I watch you
as you cuddle with sleep?
Propped on my elbow,
close, your breath brushes
back silence
like a swimmer parting water.
your lips are tight
now.
If I close my eyes
they become a cool drink
full and wet
house an active tongue
that travels my body
like an explorer
retracing familiar ground.

If I close my eyes
I can feel your tongue
dart
from my ear
to my neck
to the crevice
a prospector
pause to take samples
inspect the ore
then move on.

If I close my eyes
I can feel your tongue
wrap around my nipples
tuck them
deep
in the corner
of your mouth

and suck them
suck them
parched flowers.

If I close my eyes
oh love
if I close my eyes
I become once again
your hopeless captive
ready to submit.

I think of the
straight person who
asks what do you
do in bed?
Oh
how many times
have I
asked the same thing.

# breaking up

You'd think after spending
two years with a woman
you'd know her
you'd know what she likes to eat
and when
what she likes to wear
how she likes her hair
you'd know her favorite colors
her favorite TV shows
her favorite author
and so much more
you'd know when she's pre-menstrual
you'd know when she's uptight
you'd know when she's angry
and when she wants to fight
but then
you break up
she never liked the color blue
she never liked your gumbo
your snoring drove her crazy
she can't stand bar-be-que
she doesn't like the way you drive
she doesn't like your friends
she hates the way you comb your hair
she doesn't like her steak cooked rare
she doesn't like your politics
or anything you do

the truth it seems
in this time and place
is she really can't stand you.

You'd think after spending
two years with a woman
you'd know her
but it seems that love
like everything else
is relative.

# maybe i should have been a teacher

The next person who asks
'Have you written anything new?'
just might get hit
or at least snarled at
or cursed out.
I got a week's vacation
from work
the first
in at least two years.
The first day of vacation
I cleaned my house
scrubbed walls and floors
prepared it and me
to write.
The second day of vacation
I bought two reams of paper
a new ribbon for my typewriter
groceries to last the week.
The third day of vacation
the dog comes home
from his nocturnal run
he doesn't eat
his nose is dry
off to the vet
*parvovirus*

he'll die, no doubt,
but I doubt
been my dog
for twelve years
and I'm not ready
for him to die
so antibiotics
and broth every
two hours
and maybe he'll live.

Pick up the kid
teacher says
'she's been quiet today'
my kid is many things
at different times
what she's not
is quiet
take the kid home
temperature 100 degrees
call Alicia
'What do you do
for fever?'
aspirins, liquids,
no drafts.

So the routine begins.
Give the dog
his medicine
give the kid
her medicine
try and get
his stool for the vet
try and get
her to stay in bed
three days later
the dog is fine
the kid is fine
I'm exhausted
and it's time to
go back to work.
At work
start work on
the new protocols*
go to director's meeting
write a speech for a rally

*guidelines used by health care practitioners for patient exams.

on the weekend
lab work returns
no products of conception
call the woman
get a sonogram
she's pregnant – but
in her stomach

somebody forgot
to turn on the alarm
the we got
after being ripped
off four times
letter comes from
the IRS
I'm being audited
for 1978
they want more money
a friend calls
she's broken up
with her lover
and is afraid to get
her clothes
could I please
go with her?
she doesn't want
to call the police
I decide to go
to the bar and drink
woman decides
I'm flirting with
the bartender
who she's been
flirting with
all night

now I'm in a fight
now I'm in another fight

outside the bar
and cop cars are
coming from everywhere
and I remember
my mother telling me
I should be a teacher
and me saying
but I want to write
paint pictures
with words
read poems for people
and I get a call
from a sister
who wants me
to come read
for her college
they only have
money for advertising

and I see me
giving Ma Bell
a poster
for my January phone bill
which is huge
since I called
my friend in New York
to say I think
I'm going mad here
cause my lover
who isn't my lover
because we haven't
defined the relationship
as such
thinks we're getting
too close
seen each other
five days in a row

after the fight
we had two weeks ago
because
I had not shown
enough caring
or commitment

decides maybe
we should be
good friends
who fuck
at least
we do
that very well
and why deprive
our bodies
even if we can't
get our heads
in synch
and I think
maybe
the next person
who asks
'Have you
written anything
new?'
Just might get hit.

# child's play

Have you ever
tried to explain
human behavior
to a four-year old?
Spend the first years
saying learn to share
daughter
being selfish
self-centered
is not worthwhile
let Jamie play
with your toys
and Susie and Leotis as well.
Then Leotis decides
he should have
the pinball machine
not you
takes it away
to wherever he lives
and four-year-old tears
are asking
why
isn't Leotis sharing
my toy with me?

I want to scream
at Leotis for making
my task harder
and it doesn't matter
then
that Leotis is poor
so are we
and it doesn't matter
that
Leotis has four
brothers and sisters

I want to kill
Leotis' mother
don't understand
her
accepting toys
she didn't buy
but I can't tell
this four-year old
with tears wanting
to know why
her toy is gone
any of my anger

I calculate
the pinball machine
cost eight dollars
and pay day
is ten days away
and if I write a check
and it takes two days
to get to their bank
and then two days
to get to mine
it still has
six days to bounce.
But should I
just replace it?
there's a lesson here —
be careful of your toys
but the earlier lesson
of sharing
didn't
say *with caution*
and so I offer
a trip to the park
it's free and a diversion
and we can swing

and play on slides
and she says yes
let's go to the park.

I am angered
even more because
I know Leotis
didn't take
just a toy
he took away
some of my child's
childness.

# jonestown

As a child in Texas
race education
was simple
was subtle
was sharp

The great lone star
state sharply
placed me
in colored schools
with colored teachers
and colored books
and colored knowledge

I shopped in white stores
and bought colored clothes
'Keep the colors loud and bright
so they dazzle in the night
No matter where a nigger's bred
they love yellow, orange and red'

I used colored toilets
and rode colored buses home
I went to colored churches
with colored preachers
and prayed to a white God
begged forgiveness for Cain
and his sins
and his descendants
us lowly colored sinners
and the message
was simple
was sharp
there is a place for niggers
but not among good white folk

At home
race education
was simple
was subtle
fact gleaned
by differences

The white man
who jumped
free-fall
in the sky
was quietly dismissed
'white folks are crazy'
the white man
who turned
somersaults
on Sports Spectacular skis
was quietly dismissed
'white folks will do anything
for money'
the white man who
shot and killed his wife
and children
and then himself
received a headshake
and a sigh
and the simple statement
'white folks are crazy'

And the messages
fell into place
white folks went crazy
and went to nut houses
Black folks got mad
and went to jail
white folks owned America
Black folks built it

As I grew into adulthood
many messages were discarded
many were forgotten
but one returns to haunt me

Black folks do not commit suicide
Black folks do not
Black folks do not
Black folks do not commit suicide

November 18, 1978
more than 900 people
most of them Black
died in a man-made town
called Jonestown

Newscaster's words
slap me in my face
peoples' tears and grief
emanate from my set
and I remember the lessons
rehear a childhood message

Black folks do not commit suicide

I thought of my uncle Dave
he died in prison
suicide
the authorities said
'Boy just up and hung hisself'
and I remember my mother
her disbelief, her grief
'Them white folks kilt my brother
Dave didn't commit no suicide'
and the funeral
a bitter quiet funeral
his coffin sealed from sighters

221

and we all knew
Dave died not by his hands
some guard decided
that nigger should die

And I stare at the newscaster
he struggles to contain himself
it's a BIG BIG story
and he must not
seem too excited

'American troops made a
grizzly discovery today
in Jonestown, Guyana'
my innards scream as
the facts unfold
'a communist preacher'
and I see old Black women
my grandmothers
communist    NO
little old Black ladies
do not believe in communists
they believe in God
and Jesus     yet,
the newscasters' words
a *commune*
a media storm of
words and pictures
interviews with ex-members
survivors, city officials

the *San Francisco Chronicle*
had a problem with its presses
erratic delivery
of the morning paper
and in two days the *Chronicle*
publishes a book

*Eyewitness Account*
by a staff reporter
who survived
the airport attack
and the story grows
STEP RIGHT UP
STEP RIGHT UP
Ladies and Gentlemen
have I got a tale
for you
we got these men
two men
a congressman & a preacher
& a supporting cast of hundreds
the congressman went
to investigate the preacher
and wound up dead
the preacher wound up dead
the supporting cast
wound up dead
and all the dead
are singing to me

Black folks do not
Black folks do not
Black folks do not commit suicide

My phone rings
newscaster mistakenly says
Patricia *Parker*
not *Parks*
died on the airstrip
a friend
wants to know
are you alive?

Yes
I am here

not there
festering
in a jungle
with bloated belly
not a victim
in a dream deferred
not a piece
in a media puzzle
not a member
in the supporting cast.

Yet
I am there
walking with the souls
of Black folks
crying
screaming
WHY     WHY
Black folks
why are you here
and dead?
tell me how you
willingly died
did the minister
sing to you
'Kool-aid Kool-aid
taste great
I like Kool-aid
can't wait'

I see Black people
beautiful Black people
in lines in front of a tub
of twentieth-century hemlock
I see guards with guns
guns     guns
why guns?

and the pictures
continue to flow
images of a man
a church man
he cures disease
NO
he's a fake
hired people
treated liver
he loves God
NO
he's a communist
he talks many messages
revolution to the young
God to the old
he believes in the family
NO
he destroys the family
fucks the women
fucks the men
and the media continues
to tell the tale

An interview with a live one.
'You were a member of the People's Temple?'
'Yes, I was.'
'Why did you join?'
'Well, I went there a few times
and then I stopped going, but
Rev. Jones came by my house
and asked me why I quit coming.
I was really surprised.
No one had ever cared
that much about me before.'

No one had ever cared
that much about me before

and it came home
the messages of my youth
came clear
the Black people
in Jonestown
did not commit suicide
they were murdered
they were murdered  in
small southern towns
they were murdered in
big northern cities

they were murdered
as school children
by teachers
who didn't care
there were murdered
by policemen
who didn't care
they were murdered
by welfare workers
who didn't care
by shopkeepers
who didn't care
they were murdered
by church people
who didn't care
they were murdered
by politicians
who didn't care
they didn't die at Jonestown
they went to Jonestown dead
convinced that America
and Americans
didn't care

they died
in the schoolrooms

they died
in the streets
they died
in the bars
they died
in the jails
they died
in the churches
they died
in the welfare lines

Jim Jones was not the cause
he was the result
of 400 years
of not caring

Black folks do not
Black folks do not
Black do not commit suicide

# legacy
## for Anastasia Jean

'Anything handed down
from, or as from an
ancestor to a descendant.'

**Prologue**

There are those who think
or perhaps don't think
that children and lesbians
together can't make a family
that we create an extension
of perversion.

They think
or perhaps don't think
that we have different relationships
with our children
that instead of getting up
in the middle of the night
for a 2 AM and 6 AM feeding
we rise up and chant
'you're gonna be a dyke
you're gonna be a dyke.'

That we feed our children
lavender Similac
and by breathing our air
the children's genitals distort
and they become hermaphrodites.

They ask
'What will you say to them
what will you teach them?'

Child
that would be mine
I bring you my world
and bid it be yours.'

I

**Addie and George**

He was a small man
son of an African slave
his father came chained
in a boat
long after the boats
had 'stopped' coming
his skin was ebony
shone like new piano keys.

He was a carpenter
worked long in the trade
of the christ he chose
six days a week
his hands plied the wood
gave birth to houses
and cabinets and tables
on the seventh day
he lay down his hammer
and picked up his bible
and preached the gospel
to his brethren
led his flock in prayer

when he was seventy-nine years old
he lay down
in the presence of his wife
and children
and died.

Her father too was a slave
common law wed to an indian squaw
Addie came colored caramel
long black hair
high cheek bones.

She was a christian woman
her religion a daily occurrence
her allegiance was to God,
her husband, her children
in that order
together she and George
had twenty-two children
many never survived
the first year of life
a fact not unusual
for the time.

When she was seventy-six
George died
she began to travel
to the homes of her children
to make sure they led
a christian life
the children hid
their beer and bourbon
the grandchildren hid
she would come for two months
then move on
leave the words of Jehovah
sweating from the walls
when she was ninety-four years old
she lay down
and died.

## II
## Ernest and Marie

He came from the earth, they say,
an expression meaning *orphan*
parents in the hands of poverty
best give the boy away
and so he came to live
in a good christian home
with a good christian minister
and his wife
he was a man of many trades
roofer in the summer
tire retreader in the winter
earned far beyond
his four years of education
he wanted to see
all of his children
get educated
he lived long enough to see
his children gone and grown
and then
he lay low
and died.

She was the youngest of the twenty-two
quiet woman
tall for her time
she bore eight children
five survived the early years
she raised them in a christian way
by day she cleaned houses
by night she cleaned her own
she was sixty-two when her husband died
took her first plane trip that same year
when her third daughter was killed
she cremated her child and went home

willed herself sick and weary
she took three years to complete the task
then she lay down
and died.

**III**

It is from this past that I come
surrounded by sisters in blood
and spirit
it is this past
that I bequeath
a history of work and struggle.

Each generation improves the world
for the next.
My grandparents willed me strength.
My parents willed me pride.
I will to you rage.
I give you a world incomplete
a world where
women still
are property and chattel
where
color still
shuts doors
where
sexual choice still
threatens
but I give you
a legacy
of doers
of people who take risks
to chisel the crack wider.

Take the strength that you may
wage a long battle.

Take the pride that you can
never stand small.
Take the rage that you can
never settle for less.
These be the things I pass
to you my daughter

if this is the result of perversion
let the world stand screaming.
You will mute their voices
with your life.

# Prose

# The Demonstrator

Hey, man, what's happening? Have you made the scene yet? . . .What scene! . . .Like man ain't you hip to the battle? Ain't nobody told you about the great war that we are now waging against our white oppressors? Civil rights, man. That's what's happening, man. Like, dig, haven't you read the press on the scene in Torrance?* Yea, man, like we really upset the cats out there, man. You dig? I mean, they really lost their cool. . .What do you mean jail? Sure, if you go all the way and actually sit-in, the devils gonna bust you, but, like, CORE pays the bail and you're back on the streets in no time at all . . .What you way? . . . Mess up your job. Naw, man, this ain't like going to jail for a crime. Check this, man. There's this chick councilwoman who's trying to set things up real nice. She's trying to fix it so if you get busted behind civil rights jazz, you can still gig for the county, city, and so on. You dig? Civil service gigs for civil rights demonstrators. Heh, heh. School? Naw, man, you won't miss no time out of school. You go down on a Saturday and get busted, and CORE got you out early Sunday morning. So, Monday you make it to class and then the next weekend you ready to go down again. Hey and dig this man. You meet a lot of real cute chicks on this scene. A lotta little liberal broads who jest dying to listen to you trap to them about how bad you feel being deprived and all. Real nice broads, man. Yea. . . real nice . . . What? . . . Don't I care about the cause? Yea, man, I really dig the cause. I don't dig this separate housing, and schools and this jazz, man. No man, don't get me wrong. I'm all for the cause. I'm a stone in-te-gra-tion-ist. Yea, man, you dig. Check this, man. Those CORE cats give some boss gigs, man. They know how to get their aid. Yes . . . those cats know what's happening. So you coming down this week-end and protest with us ain't you, man? No! What you mean, man! What's the matter with you, man? Don't you believe in civil rights, man?

Like, you square, man?

*A town in California where demonstrations against housing bias have been staged.

"The Demonstrator," first appeared in *Negro Digest* in 1963.

# Autobiography Chapter One

I'm not really sure how everything happened. I mean, I started out trying to be a good kid. I really wanted my folks to like me, understand? I sure had no idea how things were going to turn out. Maybe, had I known, I could have changed something somewhere. That' s not to say I'm not a good person or anything. It's just, I do have a few quirks that not too many people can relate to, except for people like me who have the same quirks. I mean, no one starts out trying to be the family queer, but somebody's got to be. Or at least the white sheep. Black folks don't care too much for that "black sheep" business.

For a while there, it looked pretty cool for me but then my family informed me that I had to get an education. Now I have nothing against education but the people you have to get it from, Lord Jesus. Pardon the expression, but my folks were really religious and there are a few habits left from those days.

Anyway, I had to go to school and I just wasn't ready. I mean, right off in nursery school, I go, and here's this woman- a white woman at that- with a big smile on her face talking about "Now children, we must form a line and get our shots, so we don't get sick." I mean, are you ready? No one said anything to me about no needles. And the needles! I mean, I know Texas has a reputation for doing things on a giant scale, but my lord! The damn needle was longer than my arm. And that "we" crap didn't set me right either.

There wasn't much I could do about the first day but yell a lot and I did a good job of that and not without reason. Like for instance, the nurse was having one hell of a time locating our veins for the blood test. I guess she hadn't had much practice with Black kids before. And after somebody jabs you three times in the wrong place and hands you a jive smile and "Oh, I'm so sorry, dear," well any sane person doesn't want to deal with that nonsense. So right then I formulated my plan.

They used to walk through the projects where we lived and pick up each kid and we'd fall in line behind each other and march off to school. Now by the time they got to our place there was a pretty long line, and the nursery school must have had some sort of rigid schedule about starting time because they didn't waste much time waiting on any one kid. So when my mother fixed my lunch, I'd hide it. And the line would show up and there I'd be without a lunch. Well for sure, my mother wasn't going to send her baby child off to school without a lunch and the nursery school woman wasn't gonna wait while she fixed me another one. So I couldn't go to school that day.

Sometimes for diversity, I would crawl underneath my mother's bed and eat my lunch right then and there. You know how some morning you wake up with a ferocious hunger? I stopped that. One morning I was under the bed, scarfing away, and I got careless and let an apple roll out. And my mother definitely didn't think it was cute.

Once in a while I would use some of the old standards that other kids use like a stomach ache. But I did try to display some creativity in my schemes. It worked too. Nursery school was five days a week and I averaged about one day a week of attendance. After awhile, my mother got the message and since it wasn't required then, she just let me stay home. I didn't have to deal with education again until it was time for me to go to primary school. That's not to say my life got that much easier. I mean, where I grew up, kids definitely had a hard way to go, period.

Now, my mother wasn't ready for me five days a week. Not that I was not a good kid or anything, it was just my energy level was considerably higher than hers. She'd be talking about naps and I'd be scheming to get out of them. I won't go into any of my plans here. To be truthful, they didn't work. I couldn't get past those naps. One thing I did figure out, though, was if I laid down with her when she came on with, "Come on, Patty, let's take a nap" in ten minutes she'd be asleep. Then I could get up and do whatever I wanted. But most of the time I'd wind up falling asleep and blowing it.

Oh, my name is *not* Patty. That's my nickname. It's really Patricia. But I never got called that at home unless I was in trouble. There were a couple of others that they laid on me, but I'd just as soon let them remain dead. Black folks are big on nicknames.

Like I had three sisters. The first one was called "Sister" because she was the first sister. The second one was dark when she was born, so she was called "Smokey Joe" or "Smokey" and you can

239

just bet she loved that. The third one was kind of red when she was born so she was called "Red" or "Redun" which is the black way of saying "Red One". Of course as she grew up, her color changed and she was dark like the rest of us. So it'd look pretty strange for us running around calling this child "Red" but no one never thought to give her another name.

Anyway, I'm getting ahead of myself. What I was gonna tell you about was the solution of what to do with me.

My daddy had a tire shop. Actually, it was a combination of tire shop and filling station. So I was sent off to work with him and I really liked that. Obviously, no kid was gonna spend the entire day around tires and come home clean. So my mother abandoned her pleas to me of being careful and not tearing up my clothes. In fact, they gave up on dresses all together. I would spend hours climbing up and down stacks of tires.

It wasn't all good now, don't let me make that impression. My daddy was a firm believer in stuff like "Spare the rod, spoil the child", "Children should be seen and not heard" and an "Idle mind is the devil's workshop." You know, those good fun stoppers. And he was faster with the belt than any dude I've ever seen. I mean, he was a pretty big man, and I never really understood why he needed a belt in the first place. His hands were bigger than my head. And as for holding up his pants, well it didn't do much good there, either. He would put on his pants and then in less than thirty seconds, his stomach would come sneaking out over his belt. It would be less than a minute before you didn't even know he had a belt on at all.

Now my daddy was really proud of his shop. He had been working all his life for other people, ever since he quit school in the fourth grade. And he'd work hard and saved his money and now he was his own boss.

The station only had one gas pump, not like these stations now with regular this, and low-lead that, and ethyl this, and super-premium that. It had regular and ethyl in the same pump. But that was enough for his customers. Most of them couldn't buy that much gas anyway.

He made more money selling tires. He knew how to retread them, so he could sell used tires. Plenty of people bought my daddy's tires. The big problem he had was getting folks to pay for them.

Black folks sure do love their credit. I bet, if you had to pay money to get into heaven, Black folks would be at St. Peter's door talking about layaway. Anyway, it wasn't so bad.

When I first started going up there, there was this white girl about my age. Her folks owned the drug store on the corner. See, Holmon Street in Houston was sort of the big business street for Black folks at that time. The hospital where I was born was there, the elementary school I had to go to and all kinds of stores and shops. Anyway, this little girl and I used to play together. She had candy and pop from the drug store, and I had tires to crawl around in and out. So we formed a pretty good combination. At first, she was a little wimpy, but it didn't take me long to bring her around. Actually, she liked to play dolls and I didn't relate to that game at all, so we sort of compromised. She always played the mother with the baby and I was always the father so I never had to handle the baby.

I never could see what was so hot about dolls in the first place. For years, my parents would go out and buy me the biggest doll in town for Christmas and I would either lose it, break it, or trade it in the first week. I mean, first off, all the dolls were white and I felt like a fool talking about "my baby" to his blond haired, blue-eyed, piece of plastic. And the kids would change their baby's clothes, and my parents could never afford to buy me extra clothes. And sewing was a delicate art for the gifted as far as I was concerned.

Anyway, me and the drug store kid, whose name was Mary, but most of the time I called her the "drug store kid," would play every afternoon. We built houses out of tires and I would pretend I was my daddy fixing people's tires and come home with them for dinner and things. We used to have a pretty good ol' time but one day all hell broke loose. See, Mary's grandparents owned the drug store and I guess they didn't really care too much what she did as long as she didn't bother them.

Now I don't know where Mary's mama was, but one day she showed up. And Mary was with me at Daddy's shop. And when her mother found her she grabbed Mary by one arm and Mary started crying because she was really holding her tight and the mama was screaming at the grandmama about letting Mary hang around with niggers and all this time she's dragging Mary down the street. And Mary's feet were skimming along the sidewalk like rocks on the water, and my daddy was looking all mean and since he shoved me inside the shop when all the hullabaloo had started, I knew something was definitely out of order.

I was peeking around the door and Daddy was just standing there with his hands on his hips, then he came into the shop and called me over and told me I was not to play with Mary again. And me being dumb, asked him "Why not?" After I got up off the ground, he told me it was because he said so. I was to learn that this was the main reason for everything I was not supposed to do. And I never saw Mary again, after that.

"Autobiography: Chapter One," first appeared in *True to Life Adventure Stories, Volume Two*, in 1981.

# Shoes

"Gal, don't you ever do that again. You hear me?"

"Yes, daddy."

Victor released his daughter's arm and laid down his belt. Frances ran off to her room. She could hear her father still raging to her mother.

"That girl's gonna cost me all my jobs. Mr. Clark said she was downright insolent to him on the phone. She's got to understand that white folks don't like being talked to like that. They'll stop calling and then what'll we do?"

"Now Victor, calm down. She's young. She don't understand yet about these things."

"Well, dammit! She better start! It don't hurt nobody to say yessir to nobody. That girl is just too smart for her own good. Hell, she talks to me sometimes like I'm a child. All those damn teachers and books are getting to her head."

Frances turned over in her bed. She was angry. She had not done anything wrong. She had answered the phone; told the man that her father wasn't home. She'd written down his name and number, said goodbye, and hung up. The only thing she hadn't done was punctuate her sentences with sirs. Why was it so important to say sir? That was for people you respected a great deal. She didn't even know the man on the phone. For all she knew, he could have been a drinker or a gambler. Anything. She ran her fingers over her body. She could feel the sting from the belt and trace the outline of the welts beginning to form. But she didn't cry. No matter how long and hard he hit her, she wouldn't cry. And she knew that got to him. I can't stop him from whipping me, but I don't have to cry. And that gets him every time. She smiled at the thought.

Victoria cries if daddy looks at her funny. And Janice and Reba will cry if he whips them, but not me. She was tougher than any of her sisters and she was the youngest. I'll never let him see me cry.

She had come to know her father well in her ten years. In the summer, he would often take her to work with him. They moved from used-car dealer to used-car dealer. He would drag his six-foot frame from his car and put on his smile. "Howdy do, Mr. Whoever. Need any tires cut today?" And they would pause. "Well, Victor, lemme see. Yeah, I think we got a few over in the shed. Go on over and see Mr. Whoever." He would smile his grateful smile, take his stool and retreading iron, and go find Mr. Whoever. While he worked, she would amuse herself by climbing among the stacks of old tires. And when she tired of that, she would find an old magazine in one of the showrooms and sit and read. Some days there would be many tires and she would go get in her father's car and pretend she was some rich person, or an outlaw escaping jail. Some days she would be a rich king, or a lonely rich boy with no parents. Or she'd be on a big ranch with as many horses as a person could have.

At least once a month, her father would decide that he'd earned enough money to take care of his family and they would go fishing. She loved to go fishing with her father. When she was eight, he had bought her her own rod and reel. Now instead of sitting with a line and old meat hoping to snare a crab, she got to sit on the banks with him and fish like the grown-ups. Sometimes they took the rest of the family. She didn't like those times. Her sisters and mother would complain all the time about going home. When she and her father went alone, they would stay out all day and well into the night.

Those were the good times; but she also knew her father on the days when there were no tires to cut. Then the house was silent with the fear of his rage. The chickens and rabbits were inspected very carefully. If the animal's water seemed the least bit yellow, she would be whipped. Any little thing wrong and his belt would be off his waist, wrapped around his hands, and flying through the air at his target. She had seen him and felt him whip her and her sisters until her mother had grabbed him. Seen her mother stand painfully by and watch until he seemed out of control and then take him into the bedroom to find the man again. And she had learned not to cry. She was whipped more often and longer. His face would contort and his words would shatter sanity, but she would not cry. And her mother would stop him and she would lead him into their bedroom, his shoulders slumped and his step heavy. She would stand and watch, her eyes glaring, standing very tall. She would not cry, and she was the victor.

There was a new store. The vacant building behind the green pole that served as a signal for the Pioneer Bus Line to stop and pick up the black people and take them from one ward to another had been transformed into an ocean of shoes. Frances stood and peered in the window. The large cardboard figure of Buster Brown and Ty smiled back at her and she thought of the commercial. "My name's Buster Brown, I live in a shoe. This is my Dog Ty. He lives in there too."

Red and Terry approached her. "Hey Frances, let's play some peg." "Naw, I don't want to." Red and Terry were her friends. Each day after school, they would come to the bus stop and play games while waiting for the green bus to take them home. They couldn't play together in school. The boys and girls were each sent to their respective parts of the playgrounds. Frances hated playing with the other girls. They didn't like football or baseball. They only wanted to play silly girl games and giggle. But after school, she could play what she wanted. If the ground was dry, they would produce little sacks of marbles, and fire missiles into the crude circle to destroy their opponents. If the ground was wet, they would produce rusty pocket knives and play peg. They were good friends. They always returned each other's marbles, and they never tried to break each other's knife in peg.

This day she didn't want to play. She watched the man in the store put one pair of shoes here, another there. She had never seen so many different kinds of shoes. Her entire world of shoes consisted of brown-and-white saddle oxfords for school, black patent leather for Sunday, and sneakers for play. Here in this store were red shoes, blue shoes, white shoes, sandals, boots, grown-up shoes, kid shoes, the high-laced old-lady shoes, all kinds of shoes.

"Hey Frances, here comes the bus."

All the way home, Frances thought about the shoes. She imagined herself rich and having all of those shoes in her house. She watched herself changing shoes every hour and then throwing them away. She would never have to polish shoes again. She would never have to take off a pair of shoes before she could play. She could run in the mud or water and not worry about getting whipped. She wouldn't have to have taps to keep them from running over. She spent the rest of the day feeling good. Tomorrow she would get to see the shoes again.

Frances stayed after school that day and helped her teacher clean the boards and check the desks and cloakroom for forgotten articles. She knew that Red and Terry would be at the bus stop wondering where she was. But she didn't want to see them. They would want to play some game. She would take her time and let them go home. Then she could look at the shoes. They wouldn't understand if she told them about the fantasies. They would laugh. It would be better if she just let them go home.

When she reached the bus stop, they were gone. She walked to the window and looked in. She saw herself a great dancer on television wearing the blue ballet slippers. People stood up and applauded her performance, throwing roses on the stage. She took her bows and smiled.

"What are you doing?"

"Huh! Nothing... sir."

Frances looked up at the white man. She had almost forgotten, but the memory of her recent whipping swept across her mind. She had seen this man before. Yes, he was the man in the shoe shop. She smiled.

"What's your name, little girl?"

"Frances, sir."

"You live around her, Frances?"

"No, sir, I live in Sunnyside. I'm waiting for the bus."

"Sunnyside. That's a long way from here. You know how to go all that way by yourself?"

"Yessir. I do it every day. I'm a big girl now. I'm in the fifth grade."

"Would you like to come inside and look at the shoes, Frances?"

"Oh, yessir."

Frances couldn't believe what was happening. This had to be the nicest man in the world. She felt really important. It was almost like she was going to buy some shoes.

"It's almost time for me to go, so I'm going to close up the shutters, Frances. You go ahead and look around."

Frances walked slowly around the display tables. Barely touching first one shoe, then another. She would wear that shoe to the movie, and that shoe to the park, and that shoe to the rodeo, and that shoe to the circus, and-

"Would you like to go in the back and see where we store the shoes?"

"Yessir."

Frances followed the man into the little room. She stopped inside the door and he turned and beckoned her to a small stool. She sat and looked around the room. There were rows and rows of boxes. It was more fun to see the shoes in the other rom. She wondered if the man would give her a pair of shoes. He closed the door and turned to her.

"Do you like candy, Frances?"

"Yessir."

At first she hadn't noticed the man walk up to her. He had unzipped his pants and was holding a large red thing, stroking it back and forth. His eyes were funny looking, like he was nervous.

"Do you know what this is?"

"No, sir."

"Well, this is like candy, and I want you to suck it. And when you're finished, I'll give you a present."

Frances looked at the large red thing. It didn't look very much like any candy she had seen. It looked like a long, large, red mushroom. There was something white in the middle coming out of a hole. She looked at the man.

"Go on Frances, suck it."

He tilted her head and pushed the large red thing into her mouth. It felt hard and much too big. And didn't taste sweet at all like candy. The man had his hand around Frances's neck. His grip tightened.

"Suck it, up and down, like candy."

Frances was frightened. She didn't know what to do. She didn't like this candy. She didn't like the way the man sounded. His voice was mean like her father's. She felt like she was going to throw up, and was afraid she'd be beaten. All of a sudden the man let out a cry. He pulled away from her and she stared as white cream came spurting from the large red thing, which was becoming smaller. She didn't know what to do. She had knocked over the stool and backed away from the man. He had taken a handkerchief from somewhere and was wiping the red thing. He pushed it back into his pants.

"Now, didn't you like that, Frances?"

"Yessir."

"Tomorrow, after school, you come back and we'll do it again. But you mustn't tell anyone about it. It's our little game. Okay?"

"Yessir."

The man led Frances to the door. He reached into his pocket and handed her a quarter. He unlocked the front door and let her out.

"Now remember. It's our private game."

Frances didn't answer. She saw the green bus and ran to it. She didn't like the game. She looked at the quarter clutched in her hand. She dropped it on the floor of the bus.

She was very quiet that evening at home. Her mother checked her forehead to see if she had a fever. She went to bed that night and she did not think about the shoes.

The next afternoon after school, Frances talked Red and Terry into catching the bus at the next bus stop. She told them the man in the shoe store would probably take their knives if they played peg in front of his store. They never played there again.

"Shoes" first appeared in *True to Life Adventure Stories, Volume One*, in 1983.

# Mama and the Hogs

My fourth year was the beginning of an adventurous time. My family moved from the city. We moved to what is now a residential section of Houston, but then it was the country. There was our house and about two miles away was another house. We kids were really excited about this new place. There were fields and fields of blackberry bushes and no concrete in sight. There were also snakes and rats, not mice, rats and wild dogs but that didn't bother us a bit. It bothered my mother a great deal.

See, no one had told my father about the Black matriarchy. And he didn't tell my mother about buying the new house. My father was a prideful man, and he didn't like the idea of his family living in the projects. I mean for sure the houses were spacious and warm and brick, and the yards were cut and trim, but it was still the projects. And he, my father, knew this guy who just happened to have a house for sale that he could buy without a large down payment and low installments. My father had to agree to keep the man's horses, but he didn't mind at all. My mother minded.

Now we kids thought the house was great. It was made out of tin. You know the tin with waves in it. And when it rained, which it did a lot of in Houston, the drops would bounce off that tin and make such a racket that it was really great.

There were four rooms in this house. The biggest being about nine feet by twelve feet. My sisters and I all had to sleep in this one double bed. Two of us with our heads at one end and the other two at the other end. It wouldn't have been too bad, but Smokey and I hadn't quit wetting the bed, and Sister and Red weren't known for their patience and consideration. The mid-morning accidents came to be an issue of considerable passion.

The only thing I didn't like about the house was the toilet. There was none. You had to go outside to an outhouse; and when the weather was warm that's okay, but most of the time the weather was wet or cold, plus the people who build outhouses never seemed to take the size of children into consideration. Your feet never touch anything. I was always afraid I was going to lose my balance and fall in among the shit and maggots. I offered a prayer every time I had to go to the toilet.

By now you must realize that if there was no bathroom, there was no bathtub or shower. And that was okay by me; I've never been too fond of excessive amounts of water on my body. Now, I know my mother knew that my color wouldn't wash off, but sometimes it seemed like she was trying awfully hard to do that. To this day, I can't stand to scrub carrots, I empathize too much. Anyway, the bathing process was really fun. My mother had this washtub. You know the round wide tub made of some sort of metal. And she would heat water and that's how we bathed. And since there were four of us kids at home that meant she had to heat a lot of water and carry it back and forth. So the number of required baths diminished greatly. But then we had to do the washoff trip. You get a pan of water and wash your body standing up, but after a little practice, you learned to hit and miss real good. You could complete the entire process in two minutes if Mama wasn't watching. And most of the times she'd be busy doing something else.

Now my father always wanted to be a farmer, but he knew he couldn't really afford to try that with a wife and four little kids. My brother, Billy, was off in the Navy by this time. So by buying this place he could have the best of two worlds. He could go to work every day and earn money and at the same time he could raise chickens, and ducks, and rabbits and geese and guineas. A sort of mini-farm. He was able to get away with this for my entire life in Houston. After other people moved to our community, he bribed them with chickens and pig meat not to call the city about our illegal farm.

My mother on the other hand had been raised on a farm in Paris, Texas and wanted no part of another one; but she'd also been taught that a wife does what her husband wants her to. But my grandparents didn't teach her that she had to smile and be happy about it. So she very rarely smiled or was happy about this part of our lives.

First off, the house was too small. It couldn't accommodate one fourth of the furniture that we had, and my mother decided that she was not going to leave her furniture. So when we moved, all the furniture came with us. She had furniture stacked on top of each other. You could climb all the way to the ceiling which wasn't that tall to begin with and in and out of chairs and tables and vanity chests. It was great; but my mother was still bugged by our new dream castle.

Living on a farm all her life had not diminished her fear of certain animals. She could handle mice, but she couldn't deal with rats at all. I don't know how much you know about rodents, but we had what we called wood rats. Wood rats are big. No cat in its right mind would ever take one of them on.

My mother also didn't have a particular fondness for snakes either. And she didn't want to hear no shit about poisonous or not. She only related to the word snake period.

In addition to keeping the man's horses, my daddy had agreed to take care of his hogs too. And this particular job my mother really hated. In those days no one was talking about, "pigs like clean environments," so what we had was a mess of stinking hogs. And if the wind was blowing the wrong way, well, it was very difficult to cope. In a matter of a short time, my mother learned to hate those hogs. It was bad enough that she had to take care of them, but they weren't even ours. And of course kids are very good at picking up vibrations. And Sister was a master at it. She figured out that if anything were done to those hogs it wouldn't subject the culprit to a great deal of punishment.

Now the pig pen was in two parts. The first part was a little shed with a tin roof of course. And the second part was an open pen with the usual mud and feeding troughs. And there was this gate, actually, it was more like a passage way. And there was a top on it that you could lie on and the gate swung back and forth. Sister used to take Smokey and Red on top of the shed. I was too little. Then they would stomp up and down on the roof and the hogs would freak and come running out of the shed, through the gate and out into the pen. Then my sisters would lie across the gate and hit the hogs with sticks as they came through. They would do this every day.

Now there was one hog that had good sense. After the first few times, she refused to leave this shed. All the rest would still come charging out of the shed, but not this hog. She was a big mother, white with brown spots and Sister built up a real case with that hog. In fact, he became an obsession to her. She tried her damnedest to get that hog, but she just refused to leave that shed.

Smokey and Red finally got bored with the hog hitting game, but Sister would threaten them with all sorts of bodily harm to get them back on top of that shed and mess with that hog. And my mother was well aware of what they were doing, but she hated those hogs so much herself that she never stopped them or told my father about it. And the guy who owned the hogs could never figure out why his hogs were acting so strange after a while.

From time to time my mother would get so fed up that she would leave. She didn't really have any place to go, so she would just strike out walking. And we'd fall in line behind her. She'd walk up to the highway which was called the Chocolate Bayou Road. The fact that only Blacks lived in that part of town had everything to do with the name. Anyway she would take off and Sister would gather us all together and we'd go after her. We'd be crying, "Mama, Mama," and she would just be walking and crying her own self. It was a sight to see. This woman walking, actually striding, down this road and maybe fifteen feet behind her these four little kids. Yeah, it was a sight to see, except that there was no one there to see it. And after Mama walked for a ways, she'd turn around and we'd all go home. This happened about once a week. One time Mama really got mad and packed her things, told my daddy she had had it and was leaving. So we all piled in the car and off we go to the train station. She was sitting there with her arms crossed; when Mama got really mad she crossed her arms and wouldn't say anything. And we get to the station and we're all crying cause Mama is leaving and Daddy don't know what to do cause she done told him to take the house, and the animals and us and well, anyway that she had had it. I don't know what caused her to change her mind; whether it was us or daddy looking so pitiful or knowing that the minute she got back to Paris my grandparents would have sent her right back to Houston or what, but she changed her mind and left the train station and came on back with us.

But she still wasn't happy. One day she got so mad at trying to fit everything in that place that she took an axe and a sledge hammer and knocked out all the walls. So instead of five little rooms we had one big room. When my daddy got home he liked to have died. He knew for sure the whole thing was going to cave in on us, cause Mama didn't exactly redecorate according to code. But just knocking out the walls seemed to do her a world of good. And we thought it was great, cause then we could tie ropes on the rafters and play Tarzan swinging throughout the house. And Mama seemed calmer.

She also got rid of the hogs. She would go out to the pen and open the gate. And those hogs would take off with Mama and us chasing them like cowboys on a roundup or something; then she would go inside and act like she didn't know nothing about it. And the guy would come round up his hogs, but inevitably one would be missing. And he kept getting more and more confused about how his hogs kept getting away. So finally after he was losing them at a rate of one a week, he found some other place to keep them. After they were gone, Mama really got much calmer. We settled into our one room playhouse and stayed that way for the next six years of my life.

Judy Grahn provided an edited manuscript copy of "Mama and the Hogs," which was previously unpublished.

# Revolution:
# It's Not Neat or Pretty or Quick

*The following speech was given at the BASTA conference in Oak-*
*land, California, in August 1980. It represented three organi-*
*zations: The Black Women's Revolutionary Council, the Eleventh*
*Hour Battalion, and The Feminist Women's Health Center in Oak-*
*land.*

I have been to many conferences: People's Constitutional con-
vention in Washington, DC, Women's Conference on Violence in
San Francisco, Lesbian conference in Los Angeles, International
Tribunal on Crimes Against Women in Belgium. I've been to more
conferences than I can name and to many I would like to forget, but
I have never come to a conference with as much anticipation and
feeling of urgency.

We are in a critical time. Imperialist forces in the world are find-
ing themselves backed against the wall; no longer able to control
the world with the threat of force. And they are getting desperate.
And they should be desperate. What we do here this weekend and
what we take from this conference can be the difference, the decid-
ing factor as to whether a group of women will ever again be able
to meet not only in this country, but the entire world. We are facing
the most critical time in the history of the world. The super-
powers cannot afford for us to join forces and work to rid this earth
of them, and we cannot afford not to.

In order to leave here prepared to be a strong force in the fight
against imperialism we must have a clear understanding of what
imperialism is and how it manifests itself in our lives. It is perhaps
easier for us to understand the nature of imperialism when we look
at how this country deals with other countries. It doesn't take a
great amount of political sophistication to see how the interest of
oil companies played a role in our relationship with the Shah's Iran.
The people of Iran were exploited in order for Americans to drive
gas-guzzling monsters. And that is perhaps the difficult part of im-
perialism for us to understand.

The rest of the world is being exploited in order to maintain our standard of living. We who are 5 percent of the world's population use 40 percent of the world's oil.

As anti-imperialists we must be prepared to destroy all imperialist governments, and we must realize that by doing this we will drastically alter the standard of living that we now enjoy. We cannot talk on one hand about making revolution in this country, yet be unwilling to give up our videotape records and recreational vehicles. An anti-imperialist understands the exploitation of the working class, understands that in order for capitalism to function, there must be a certain percentage that is unemployed. We must also define our friends and enemies based on their stand on imperialism.

At this time, the super powers are in a state of decline. The Iranians rose up and said no to U. S. imperialism; the Afghanis and Eritreans are saying no to Soviet-social imperialism. The situation has become critical and the only resource left is world war between the U.S. and the Soviet Union. We are daily being given warning that war is imminent. To some people, this is no significant change, just escalation. The Blacks, poor whites, Chicanos, and other oppressed people of this country already know we're at war.

And the rest of the country's people are being prepared. The media is bombarding us with patriotic declarations about "our" hostages and "our" embassy in Iran. This government is constantly reminding us of our commitment to our allies in Israel. Ads inviting us to become the few, the chosen, the marine or fly with the air force, etc. are filling our television screens.

And it doesn't stop there. This system is insidious in its machinations. It's no coincidence that the "right wing" of this country is being mobilized. Media sources are bombarding us with the news of KKK and Nazi party activity. But we who were involved in the civil rights movement are very familiar with these tactics. We remember the revelations of FBI agents, not only infiltrating the Klan but participating in and leading their activities. And we are not for one moment fooled by these manipulations.

The Klan and the Nazis are our enemies and must be stopped, but to simply mobilize around stopping them is not enough. They are functionaries, tools of this governmental system. They serve in the same ways as our armed forces and police. To end Klan or Nazi activity doesn't end imperialism. It doesn't end institutional racism; it doesn't end sexism; it does not bring this monster down, and we must not forget what our goals are and who our enemies are. To simply label these people as lunatic fringes and not accurately assess their roles as a part of this system is a dangerous error. These people do the dirty work. They are the arms and legs of the congressmen, the businessmen, the Tri-lateral Commission.

And the message they bring is coming clear. Be a good American—Support registration for the draft. The equation is being laid out in front of us. Good American= Support imperialism and war.

To this, I must declare—I am not a good American. I do not wish to have the world colonized, bombarded and plundered in order to eat steak.

Each time a national liberation victory is won I applaud and support it. It means we are one step closer to ending the madness that we live under. It means we weaken the chains that are binding the world.

Yet to support national liberation struggles alone is not enough. We must actively fight within the confines of this country to bring it down. I am not prepared to let other nationalities do my dirty work for me. I want the people of Iran to be free. I want the people of Puerto Rico to be free, but I am a revolutionary feminist because I want me to be free. And it is critically important to me that you who are here, that your commitment to revolution is based on the fact that you want revolution for yourself.

In order for revolution to be possible, and revolution *is* possible, it must be led by the poor and working class people of this country. Our interest does not lie with being a part of this system, and our tendencies to be co-opted and diverted are lessened by the realization of our oppression. We know and understand that our oppression is not simply a question of nationality but that poor and working class people are oppressed throughout the world by the imperialist powers.

We as women face a particular oppression, not in a vacuum but as a part of this corrupt system. The issues of women are the issues of the working class as well. By not having this understanding, the women's movement has allowed itself to be co-opted and misdirected.

It is unthinkable to me as a revolutionary feminist that some women's liberationist would entertain the notion that women should be drafted in exchange for passage of the ERA. This is a clear example of not understanding imperialism and not basing one's political line on its destruction. If the passage of the ERA means that I am going to become an equal participant in the exploitation of the world; that I am going to bear arms against other Third World people who are fighting to reclaim what is rightfully theirs—then I say Fuck the ERA.

One of the difficult questions for us to understand is just "what is revolution?" Perhaps we have had too many years of media madness with "revolutionary eye make-up and revolutionary tampons." Perhaps we have had too many years of Hollywood fantasy where the revolutionary man kills his enemies and walks off into the sunset with his revolutionary woman who has been waiting for his return. And that's the end of the tale.

The reality is that revolution is not a one-step process: you fight- you win- it's over. It takes years. Long after the smoke of the last gun has faded away the struggle to build a society that is classless, that has no traces of sexism and racism in it, will still be going on. We have many examples of societies in our lifetime that have had successful armed revolution. And we have no examples of any country that has completed the revolutionary process. Is Russia now the society that Marx and Lenin dreamed? Is China the society that Mao dreamed? Before and after armed revolution there must be education, and analysis, and struggle. If not, and even if so, one will be faced with coups, counter-revolution and revision.

The other illusion is that revolution is neat. It's not neat or pretty or quick. It is a long dirty process. We will be faced with decisions that are not easy. We will have to consider the deaths of friends and family. We will be faced with the decisions of killing members of our own race.

Another illusion that we suffer under in this country is that a single facet of the population can make revolution. Black people alone cannot make a revolution in this country. Native American people alone cannot make revolution in this country. Chicanos alone cannot make revolution in this country. White people alone cannot make revolution in this country. Women alone cannot make revolution in this country. Gay people alone cannot make revolution in this country. And anyone who tries it will not be successful.

Yet it is critically important for women to take a leadership role in this struggle. And I do not mean leading the way to the coffee machine.

A part of the task charged to us this weekend is deciding the direction we must take. First I say let us reclaim our movement. For too long I have watched the white middle class be represented as my leaders in the women's movement. I have often heard that the women's movement is a white middle class movement.

I am a feminist. I am neither white nor middle class. And the women that I've worked with were like me. Yet I am told that we don't exist, and that we didn't exist. Now I understand that the racism and classism of some women in the movement prevented them from seeing me and people like me. But I also understand that with the aid of the media many middle class women were made more visible. And this gave them an opportunity to use their skills gained through their privilege to lead the movement into at first reformist and now counter-revolutionary bullshit.

These women allowed themselves to be red-baited and dyke-baited into isolating and ignoring the progressive elements of the women's movement. And I, for one, am no longer willing to watch a group of self-serving reformist idiots continue to abort the demands of revolutionary thinking women. You and I are the women's movement. It's leadership and direction should come from us.

We are charged with the task of rebuilding and revitalizing the dreams of the 60s and turning it into the reality of the 80s. And it will not be easy. At the same time that we must weed reformist elements out of our movement we will have to fight tooth and nail with our brothers and sisters of the left. For in reality, we are "all products of a decadent capitalist society."

At the same time that we must understand and support the men and women of national liberation struggles—the left must give up its undying loyalty to the nuclear family. In the same way it is difficult for upper and middle class women to give up their commitment to the nuclear family, but the nuclear family is the basic unit of capitalism and in order for us to move to revolution it has to be destroyed. And I mean destroyed. The male left has duped too may women with cries of genocide into believing it is revolutionary to be bound to babies. As to the question of abortion, I am appalled at the presumptions of men. The question is whether or not we have control of our bodies which in turn means control of our community and its growth. I believe that Black women are as intelligent as white women and we know when to have babies or not. And I want no man regardless of color to tell me when and where to bear children. As long as women are bound by the nuclear family structure we cannot effectively move toward revolution. And if women don't move, it will not happen.

We do not have an easy task before us. At this conference we will disagree; we will get angry; we will fight. This is good and should be welcomed. Here is where we should air our differences but here is also where we should build. In order to survive in this world we must make a commitment to change it; not reform it—revolutionize it. Here is where we begin to build a new women's movement, not one easily co-opted and mis-directed by media pigs and agents of this insidious imperialist system. Here is where we begin to build a revolutionary force of women. Judy Grahn in the "She Who" poems says, "When she who moves, the earth will turn over." You and I are the she who and if we dare to struggle, dare to win, this earth will turn over.

"Revolution: It's Not Neat or Pretty or Quick," was first delivered as a speech as indicated in the head note; this fair transcription first appeared in *This Bridge Called My Back: Writings by Radical Women of Color*, in 1983.

# Poetry at Women's Music Festivals: Oil and Water

My presence at the National Women's Music Festival surprised many women. As I walked the grounds during the day prior to my performance, I was often met with, "Oh, how nice to see you," followed in rapid succession by "What are you doing here?"

I was neither surprised nor angered by this response, but somewhat disappointed that the battle I have been waging for the last 20 years is still not finished.

It seems that there are people who believe that the combination of poetry and music, like oil and water, simply cannot mix, and to carry that combination to a concert stage is unfathomable. The belief carries with it certain unsupported conclusions: that poetry cannot stand alone as a performing art and will be automatically overwhelmed by any music with perhaps the exception of light classical; that audiences will not come out in large numbers for poetry; that even the audience that does come out can only tolerate a small amount of poetry in a sitting, definitely no more than 15 to 20 minutes.

For more than 20 years I have been fighting to destroy these myths, lay them like so many others women have struggled against: women become unstable when pre-menstrual and thus cannot be placed in positions of authority and power; a woman is not complete unless she has given birth. I want to lay them in a deeply-buried tomb out of our existence.

It is not difficult to understand the resistance to the idea of poetry as a performing art. For years our concept of poetry and its presentation has been dominated by male academic ivory towerites. We have been conditioned to find poetry isolated and secluded from the masses of people, a pursuit only to be understood and especially enjoyed by those who possess trained minds and favored breeding. It has long been touted as an art form to be admired for its stylistic machinations with severe limitations on its concepts and subject matter.

Many of us sat in classrooms across this country and were told by balding men in tweed jackets, sisters in black habits, or high-collared women exactly what poetry was and how it was to be read. We were forced to memorize poems of bloody but unbowed heads, multi-faceted love, and mothers' hopes for their sons. We left those classrooms for the most part turned off by the clinical dissection of words to the point of sterility.

Some of us left those rooms and have never since looked between the covers of a book of poetry or crossed the threshold of a room where poetry was being read. Some of us, in spite of the antiseptic approach to the art, developed and retained a love for poetry; we were able to get past the archaic rituals and see the beauty and power of honing thought to its bare essence.

Yet we also took with the art form the trappings that surrounded it. We were content to go into sterile university poetry centers and dimly-lit coffeehouses and sit on hard, straight chairs and support-less sofas to listen to poets: young brash poets, old alcoholic poets, women in long skirts with straight long hair. They were almost always white and almost always men.

In the 1960s, things began to change. Hundreds of thousands of people took to the streets and began voicing other concerns. Concerns that touched our lives: a war in a far-away pace with an unknown people; the separateness of America's ethnic minorities and inequality of her perceptions of them; the role of women and the rape of our minds and bodies.

The poets and poetry also changed. The concerns voiced by people in the streets appeared on pages clutched by angry hands. The audiences and the forums also began changing. Women poets started leaving the university reading rooms and coffeehouses and began going to women's centers. The move toward consciousness had created a different need and a new way to approach poetry and its presentation.

Women's centers, which in many instances were represented by a single night allocated to women in the backroom of a coffeehouse or YWCA, started sponsoring poetry reading.

Women began applying the lessons learned in consciousness-raising work and to their approach to other writers. The competi-tiveness and the one-upmanship of the male poetry scene was re-placed by a joyful sharing of ideas and a commitment to sisterhood. The antagonistic discussions between poets regarding who was published and who was not and by whom; how many chapbooks poets had to their credit; and who should read last (the honored position) in a reading were replaced by discussions about the need for more presses, feminist publishers, and women's spaces to promote the work of all as opposed to a few.

Yet even as we moved away from the past, we still refused to let go of all the rituals. Our poetry readings were all women poets and all women audiences, yet we still believed poetry to be a quiet, passive art form to be read in small rooms with other poets. On occasion the sets would be shared with musicians, and then only one musician usually playing a guitar.

In the early 1970s I convinced a bar owner in San Francisco (actually a local bar owner's girlfriend) to bring poetry into the bar, but not before hearing all of the usual objections: bar women would not sit still for poetry, bar women would not give up their junkboxes and pool tables for poetry, and so forth. But eventually a compromise was struck that would alter my life.

We agreed to have the shows on Sunday afternoons, a historically slow time for the bar. We also agreed to four 20-minute sets: two poetry, two music. Finding the musicians was easy; finding poets who were willing to stand on a pool table covered with plywood and read to a bar of dykes while strictly adhering to a 20-minute time limit was almost impossible.

The first Sunday was met with curiosity, and the audience was more one of place and circumstance than of desire to view the performances, but word spread. Soon Sunday afternoons became one of the more popular times to attend that bar, and I became convinced of the fusion of women's music and poetry was a powerful combination that would do more to the raising of women's consciousness than either poet or musician could hope to accomplish singularly.

In the mid '70s, poet Judy Grahn was approached by the women of Olivia Records to record an album. She asked me to record with her, and *Where Would I Be Without You* was completed in August of 1976. This opened up another door.

The women of Olivia wanted to produce shows featuring their recording artists, and Judy and I were Olivia artists. So negotiations were begun. One major snag was over the performers' fees. Someone put forth the idea that since musicians had to rehearse they should be paid more than the poets. The poets put forth that they had been rehearsing their entire lives for those poems. The matter was settled, and the combination of poets and musicians took to the auditorium stage.

"Women on Wheels" produced several concerts and the "Varied Voices of Black Women" took to the road during 1977 and 1978. Thousands of women saw and felt the experience. It had been proven successfully that the combination worked. Women who had convinced themselves that they hated poetry were reintroduced to the art form and loved it. Women who loved poetry but were totally unaware of women's music heard it and loved it.

Even with the evidence before us we still tried to deny the feasibility of the two forms coexisting on stage. Women's music festivals were flourishing over the country, and there was one very large absence: poetry. The same arguments that were voiced 15 years ago were being repeated.

Thus I was not surprised by the reactions of women in Bloomington this year to a poet in their midst. There has not been enough experience for them to realize and feel comfortable with the idea that poets and poetry belong at women's festivals.

It is not easy even with consciousness to discard the environmental trappings that accompany most art forms. Most of us still expect to see classical musicians in white blouses and long black skirts—but we are changing and growing.

I was also not surprised by the reactions of women following my performance in Bloomington. One woman in the stage crew ran up and exclaimed, "They're standing up; they're giving you a standing ovation." the surprise in her voice told me that she had never seen a poetry performance; she had never felt the energy reverberate through a room with the Audre Lordes, Adrienne Richs, and Judy Grahns of this world. The glow in her face also told me that she would do so in the future.

Many women approached me in the days following my performance, wanting to know why I hadn't been at this festival before and when I was coming to that one. The answers to those questions do not lie with me. We still have many myths to bury and many biases to change. Producers feel—and rightfully so—that they have an obligation to provide entertainment that women want and will like, and the last they checked we "didn't like poetry."

So, to those who would still doubt the mix of poetry and music, I would remind them of the ingredients needed for Good Seasons salad dressing mix: spices, vinegar, oil and water.

"Poetry at Women's Music Festivals: Oil and Water" first appeared in *Hot Wire* in 1986.

# Gay Parenting, Or, Look out, Anita

Five years ago, my lover Marty and I decided we wanted to raise a child together. This in itself did not seem so earthshaking, and it wasn't. It was complicated by the fact that we are both women. It shouldn't have been, but it was.

The first discussions evolved around the process. How do we get a child? I have long been an advocate of adoption. It seems logical to me that you take a child who needs a parent and a parent who wants a child and make two people happy. However, we had to look at reality. The chances of us getting a healthy infant through the state adoption system, even in the reputably liberal state of California, was not going to be easy. I had once been warned by a lesbian friend in a position of power in the organization to go into the closet if I wanted to become a "Big Sister". Now my closet door has no key; it's impossible for me to go lock myself in it. We decided that the logical decision was for one of us to become pregnant and have the child.

At the time, I was thirty-eight years old and worked full-time as director of the Oakland Feminist Women's Health Center, as well as being a writer and a performer. Many of the staff at the health center had had children recently. So many, in fact, that we set up a child-care center in the building. That way, our staff could still bring their babies to work but not have them crawling all over the place. Having a baby would clearly not interfere with my job at the clinic. However, the image of myself appearing pregnant on stage did not appeal to me. In fact, the image of me appearing pregnant anywhere did not appeal to me, and the prospect of childbirth was downright unattractive.

So, it seemed Marty would be the candidate for birthing. Unfortunately, that also presented a problem. Marty is a journeywoman roofer. No way was she going to be climbing ladders with eighty-pound sacks, pregnant. We calculated when the rainy or off-season for roofers would be, and then calculated when she would need to conceive to deliver during that time. Of course, lingering in the back of both of our minds was the realization that with conception, no one has any guarantees.

The next consideration was race. I am Black; Marty is white. I was already coparenting an all-white child with an ex-lover, and I definitely wanted this child to be at least half-Black. At the same time, I had to consider the possibility that if I died, the raising of the child would be left to Marty. In recent years, I have seen several white women raising half-Black children white. I definitely wanted no part of that phenomenon. Would Marty be able to raise our child and give her a sense not only of culture, but also of identity, without me? Marty is a feminist. She knows and understands oppression, and dealing with racism is a constant part of her political process. She could, and more importantly would, raise our child with political consciousness.

The next question was, "Who's going to be the biological father?" This presented problems. We definitely wanted to raise this child. We did not want to find ourselves in court a year or two later fighting the biological father because he decided he wanted to be a parent. And we were both too feminist to simply have Marty go out and pick up some stranger.

Fortunately, the health center had started the Northern California Sperm Bank, which has a donor insemination program as one of its components. Marty and I would be able to go to the sperm bank as a couple, screen the donor catalog, and pick a donor. I could be present at the insemination or do it myself. This solved the legal problem of having the birth father turn up later in our lives and eliminated the concern about the health of the biological father. The sperm bank extensively screens their donors. A donor being accepted would mean we would not only have a complete past medical history, but current screening for AIDS, gonorrhea, and a host of other illnesses and diseases. Plus we would be able to pick a donor as near as possible to my physical characteristics. The combination of feminism with modern technology is awesome.

All that was needed now was to register with the sperm bank, go through the orientation program, and wait for the right time to begin insemination. While Marty was willing to be the birth mother, she had no overwhelming desire to experience the "miracle of childbirth." It simply seemed the best way to accomplish our goal. But the goddess was watching out for us.

In January 1983, I received a call from a woman who runs a private adoption agency. She had a sixteen-year old Black woman who was almost seven months pregnant, and she had no Black couples on the waiting list. She wanted to know if our health center knew of any couples. I knew for sure of me. I told the woman I would call her back.

Marty then gets an excited me saying "There's this sixteen-year old, pregnant, Black, wants to give the child up but needs to live with the adoptive parents until she delivers because no one knows she's pregnant except her mother and what do you think? Yeah, right."

Marty thought. "Yeah."

I called back the adoption agency and told the counselor to see if the young woman was interested in single parent adoption. At that time, two people of the same sex couldn't adopt a child in California. The report came back, "Fine," and arrangements were made for Marty and me to meet with the birth mother (who I'll call Mary) and her mother (who I'll call Jane) to decide if she would be comfortable living with us and if we would be comfortable having her live with us.

Now, if you want to put your house in order, adopt a child. Walls were painted, floors were stripped, stained, and verithaned, and new curtains bought. All the things you say you are going to do someday get done.

Mary and Jane came to our house. My stereotypical fears about the "fast" teenager were quickly dismissed. Mary was a sweet kid. She was a quiet, bright girl, who unfortunately succumbed to peer pressure and got caught. When the adoption counselor had told me about them, I admit I was skeptical about Mom. How do you have a six-month pregnant daughter and not notice? Jane worked at night and was unaware of Mary's condition until it was too late to have an abortion. This was aided by the fact that at six months pregnant, Mary weighed 105 pounds. I took her to buy maternity clothes, and they practically laughed us out of the store. The smallest size they had hung on her. She went through her entire pregnancy in her regular jeans with the top two buttons undone. Jane was very supportive of her daughter. She allowed her to make the decision whether or not to raise her baby.

Living with Mary was an incredible experience. Marty and I were elated over the fact that we were soon going to have our baby, and yet at the same time we had to be sensitive to Mary's feelings. So things were kept low keyed for the most part. At the same time, we were living with a teen-ager. I discovered a whole new set of television shows, learned that I liked rap music, and finally put my foot down on going to horror movies. Anastasia (our daughter) is almost four-years old, and Marty still talks about those movies.

Most of our conversations were about Mary's future, her present studies (we had a tutor come in to prevent her from falling behind), how she was going to handle her peer group when she returned to school, and what her plans were for college.

At the same time, we needed to be realistic. In a short amount of time, Mary was going to have a baby. I took her to the obstetrician, had one of the birthing counselors from the health center come over and instruct her in prenatal exercises, labor, and delivery. I also managed to convince her that even though hamburgers, French fries, and Coke tasted good, there were other foods. By the time Mary left our house, she was converted to lobster, crab, and pinochle.

Finally, the time came. After one episode of Braxton-Hicks contractions (false labor), Mary was ready to deliver our baby. The physician (one of our health center doctors) had prearranged everything with the hospital; so off went Mary, Jane, Marty and I for the delivery. The nurses weren't quite sure how to handle the situation, but they did well.

No matter how much preparation, education, and counseling, sixteen-year old children are not ready for childbirth. Having babies hurts, and watching Jane watch her baby have a baby, was not easy. Marty coached Jane, and I coached Mary, and Anastasia (Stasia for short) was born. Following the delivery, we moved Mary off the maternity ward to a private room, and for the next three days post delivery, I went to the hospital and fed Anastasia at 2:00, 6:00, and 10:00 am and pm. I was tired and bleary-eyed, but very happy.

In three days, Mary went home to Jane, and Anastasia came home to us. Jane brought us flowers and wished us well with our new baby. We were parents.

Even in private adoptions, you must be approved by the State. We had a caseworker come to our home three times (usually it's two visits) and she visited Jane four times (usually it's one home visit and one office visit). This woman wanted to make sure that Jane knew she was giving up her child to a couple of lesbians, even if only my name appeared on the papers. She knew. After nine months of visits, the final papers were signed and the adoption was final.

In raising our child, we have had to do some serious consciousness-raising among family and friends. Anastasia was our child, neither mine alone nor Marty's alone. She has two mothers. One of Marty's sisters-in-law asked us, "What will she call you?" She seemed greatly relieved to know that neither of us would be called Daddy.

The family structure we utilized is not new. Extended families have always existed in Black culture. We simply modified it slightly. Marty's folks are her grandparents. My parents are dead. My ex-lover's parents (remember I'm coparenting another child) are also her grandparents. My other daughter is her sister. All brothers and sisters (Marty's and mine) are uncles and aunts and their siblings are cousins. In addition, she has one godmother (white) and two godfathers (Black).

This was not difficult to accomplish. We simply made it clear that anyone wishing to participate in this child's life had to accept the premise that she has two mothers. In her first three years, Anastasia has been to southern California to see my family several times, met her great-aunt from Texas, made two trips to Ohio (Marty's parents), one being a family reunion, and is watched regularly by her aunt in Berkeley (Marty's sister) and her aunt in Oakland (my ex-lover). Our biggest problem is making sure that we visit everyone fairly equally, given distance and cost considerations.

It's amazing. Relatives may not understand or be comfortable with lesbians, but they do understand *baby*. A little over two years ago, we decided to buy a home in the suburbs. Stasia's grandfather's (Marty's father) concern was that there might be some racist or homophobe in the neighborhood who would try to cause harm to his grandchild. So to appease her father, Marty went around to all the houses on our block and informed the occupants that we were thinking about buying a house in their neighborhood, and if they had any problems with to say so, please, before we bought the house. None of the neighbors seemed upset about our family structure, but a few did look at Marty strangely for a while.

Raising Stasia has not been uncomplicated, but I know for sure it has been easier than what my friends had to go through twenty years ago. We have the benefit of the civil rights movement, the gay liberation movement, and the feminist movement. We also have the advantage of both being women who spent a lot of time around children. There was no need for lessons to change diapers or prepare bottles. Anastasia's diaper was changed by whoever discovered it needed to be changed. Her late-night feeding was done by whoever was less tired. Since our work was equally important to both of us, it naturally evolved that if I needed to bring work home or was writing, Marty took care of Stasia and I, in turn, do the same. She's taken to the doctor for her check-ups by whoever can most easily get free.

Marty and I come from two different races, classes, and cultures, and we knew that at some point in time, we would disagree about how the other was dealing with Stasia. So we agreed before she was born to never criticize each other about how we were handling a situation with Anastasia in front of her. This was one of the lessons I learned from my ex-lover. It saves us. In addition to minimizing Anastasia's opportunity to play one of us against the other, it also means we constantly talk about rearing our child. She knows my ideas around childrearing. I know her ideas around childrearing.

Thousands of lesbians have reared children before us, and thousands will after us, but one major difference in Anastasia's life is that she is not being raised "heterosexual."

I've seen lesbians with their children who try to "out-straight" the straight folks. I know one woman whose daughter's entire wardrobe is pink. I've seen women allow their male children to go shirtless in hot weather, but not their daughters, with no discussion of male privilege. The girls get dolls; the boys get trucks. In our house, Anastasia gets almost everything. No war toys, guns, racist, or sexist books allowed.

Most importantly, she gets positive images. She knows women can work on roofs and at computers. Women can cook and clean houses, cut yards and build fences. Women play chess and Scrabble; they also fish and play softball.

The learning doesn't just occur at home. We had to educate her teachers as well. She attends a Montessori school. We put her there because of their progressive reputation. They got it that she would get picked up by both of us; that the permission slip was signed by whoever remembered to do it; that potluck-food was prepared by whoever had time. I still had to go to the school after her first Mother's Day there and make it clear that she came home with two Mother's Day gifts or none at all. They've learned that one, and I must give them credit. At least they had the good sense not to send her home with a Father's Day present.

Anastasia knows she has two mothers, and because of the changing familial structure in this country, she's not at all unusual. She has friends with one parent, two parents, three parents, and four parents. She doesn't have to fear that her playmates will ostracize her because her parents are lesbians. Many of her friend's parents are lesbians and gay men, and those who are not, know who she is and who we are. The only closets in our house hold clothes.

Anastasia will soon be four years old. She knows the difference between boys' bodies and girls' bodies. She knows that Marty is one race and I am another. She has no idea what sexual preference is, but she knows her godfather Joe loves Julie, and her godfather Charles loves Pablo. She also knows that her mama Pat loves her mama Marty and they both love her. Her friends and loved ones are all races and classes.

We still have a long way to go in eliminating the things that oppress people in this society, but we are trying to change them, and we know that one of the ways to do this is to teach the children. The thing that is exciting about our child's life is that she is not alone in her learnings.

People, get ready! If you are racist, sexist, classist, or homophobic, my child is going to think you are strange.


"Gay Parenting, Or, Look Out, Anita" first appeared in *Politics of the Heart: A Lesbian Parenting Anthology* in 1987.

# The 1987 March on Washington: The Morning Rally

When HOT WIRE editor Toni Armstrong asked me if I'd be willing to do an article about the 1987 March on Washington—specifically the "Third World Rally" and what it meant a year later—I quickly said, "Yes, no problem."

No problem, indeed. Since that phone conversation, I have paced a quarter-inch groove in my studio carpet, chewed enough toothpicks to make a three-year-old redwood tree, and generally became a royal expletive deleted.

**Some of the Morning Rally Participants Included**

Pat Parker
Shelley Ettinger
Pat Norman & Hilda Mason
Renee McCoy
Faith Nolan
Lifeline
Kwanza
Connie Panzarino
Kathy Tsui
Buffy Denker
Tana Loi
Ginitta & Friends
Native American prayer ceremony
Lavender Light Gospel Choir

Looking back to the March conjured up all the mixed emotions that existed for me then: the sense of having traveled so far and yet having so far to go, while at the same time passing by lush meadows and crystal blue lakes that entice one to stop and rest and abandon the journey.

The circumstances that brought me to Washington on that cold October day had given me cause to worry. I received a phone call from Pat Norman, who was serving as one of the national co-chairs of the March. It seemed that Pat had been doing battle. The power that be—the individuals responsible for the logistics of the March, who we shall hereafter refer to as the G.O.B. (read gay old boys)—had once again overlooked the participation of third world people. A compromise was made, and the "Morning Rally" was the result.

Pat Norman sounded tired on the phone that afternoon. "Parker, I want you heard," she told me. "These people need to hear what you have to say." I agreed to come to Washington, but I was conflicted. In 1970, I and a few other women had made forays into the male-dominated gay liberation movement. The goal was unity and coalition. The result was frustration, anger, and rage. There were certain factors that we as lesbians had not considered. One, that men—not unlike women—come to the gay life for different reasons: some because they love their same sex; others because they hate the opposite sex. Two, that a white gay man in the closet enjoyed all the privileges of this patriarchal society, and he was not about to give them up easily.

So we found ourselves exhausting valuable time and energy in arguments over the rights of drag queens, the word "girl," and numerous other issues that brought us no closer together—and in fact sent the lesbians out the door angry and disgusted, swearing that the male gay movement was "not ready."

Those memories were fresh in my mind, coupled with the experiences of being a lesbian of color in both the feminist and gay movements. I kept reminding myself that 1970 was almost twenty years ago and times had changed; that the myopic tendencies of the G.O.B. was limited to a few and not the many.

The other part of me wanted to be in Washington. The memory of the 1968 March on Washington led by the Black civil rights movement was vivid. I had not gone to that march because, like so many people in the country at the time, I simply could not afford it, and I am too much of a Capricorn child to put my finger in the wind and take a chance on where I will lay my head down at night. Yet I was well aware of the ramifications of participating in an event of that magnitude. I have talked often with people who participated in that March, and it still affects them to this day. The rumblings through the grapevine here indicated that this March on Washington would be similar in its effect on people.

So, I boarded a plane last October and headed for the District of Columbia. On the plane from San Francisco to O'Hare Airport in Chicago, there were several small clusters of gay men and lesbians, about twenty in all. The gay-appearing (and note here that what appears "gay" to gay people and "gay" to straight people are a world apart) service representative who took our tickets handed them back with a knowing smile and said, "I know where you're going."

Switching planes in Chicago and boarding the flight to Washington drastically changed the numerical make-up of the passengers. Now the plane was approximately twenty-five percent gay, and the somber passengers who read their books and magazines between San Francisco and Chicago started exchanging names and learning the place of origin of their sister and fellow passengers. The mood lifted, and excitement and anticipation permeated the atmosphere.

Washington D.C. was packed. Gay mean and lesbians were everywhere. The proportion of men to women, however, seemed to me to be greatly imbalanced, pointing up once again the great difference in the economic realities between men and women. That same economic imbalance was evident in the proportion of whites to people of color. In spite of this, the feeling of community and power was covering the city like a comforter. Washington was, for those few days, a gay town. The streets, restaurants, hotels, and parks were peopled by queers. And the sense of power that comes with numbers—plus the realization for some that they were a long way from home, and their parents and bosses were not watching—led to a mass exodus from the closets. People blatantly walked, strolled, and strutted through the streets of our nation's capital holding hands, arms around shoulders with no fear, no turning of hands to spot the enemy. And the enemy was silent. The occasional bold soul who dared to scream out "faggot" or "queer" was immediately surrounded by bodies screaming back, "Yeah, and what are you going to do about it?"

The sense of power was infectious. I flashed back to a time early in the movement when the idea was put forth of founding a lesbian state, a place where we could live in peace and without closets. At that time I said "no way." I was not prepared to live in a totally lesbian state, because to the gay movement I was still invisible. (Although I feel more visible today, I still believe that no minority can make major change alone; when we join together we create power blocks and become a force to be reckoned with.) And to those in the early days who were aware of people of color, many equated third world lesbians with violence, drugs, booze, hustlers, and poverty.

In speaking of the feminist and lesbian-feminist movements, many still say that they are "white women's movements"—yet I was there and have never been white. Still for a few days in that October of 1987 I considered the possibility that maybe such a thing was now viable. Faggots and dykes of different races and cultures reveled in their togetherness; embraced each other without reservation.

October 8th arrived, and the early morning streets were filled with people. The morning rally—which has mistakenly since been dubbed the "Third World rally"—was to begin at 9 a.m., following the reading of the Names Project quilt. The people involved in setting up the morning rally sought to fill in the obvious gaps in the program of the main rally, which was scheduled to follow the March. The morning rally producers sought to bring together not only representatives of the third world, but also people who had been there when no one else was. A major criticism that can be levied against our movement today is our glaring failure to teach our history to those who follow, and to honor those who stood alone.

I was honored to share the stage with early activists such as Morris Kight and Buffy Dunker. I went to Washington knowing that Pat Norman had not asked me to come just because she liked my poetry, but because she knew that back in the late '60s and early '70s I took my words into church and bars, coffeehouses, and parks and said, "I am Black and I am Lesbian; I am proud of both and not willing to compromise either." Pat Norman knew that I had stood alone.

So I was filled with mixed emotions that day. I was exhilarated by the signs of hundreds of thousands of lesbians and gay men gathering to march through the streets of Washington; I was honored when Pat took my hand, led me to the front of the March, and said, "You march here; you deserve it." Yet I was saddened by the fact that so many who deserved to be there were not.

As I walked through those streets, filled with pride, I couldn't help but ask, where is Judy Grahn? She was there in the early '70s breaking new ground—why is she not here? As I watched the main rally, I was thrilled to see people like Whoopi Goldberg risking the wrath of the neo-fascists in our midst and risking monetary losses and damage to her career—but where was Audre Lorde? She did the same thing almost fifteen years ago.

As I watched performer after performer take the stage, I could not help but remember Paul Mariah, a white gay man who took his poems to the straight poetry readings (the only forum available) and tolerated the polite indifference of his peers to the pain and isolation chronicled in his work.

Despite what was missing, I could not help but feel pride as I watched an event unfold that had been a dream. I could not help but leave Washington filled with hope and expectation of what was to follow. I knew that so many of those people who had never dared to leave their closets would find it extremely difficult to go back into them when they returned home. I knew that so many of the doubts and mistrusts of various gay groups toward each other had been broken down. I knew that hundreds of thousands of lesbians and gay men, buoyed by the energy of that march, had left that town filled with the commitment to continue to struggle for change. I believed that the straight world had best brace itself, for returning into their midst was an army of people who not only believed but knew that they had the right to exist and live their lives openly and without shame.

So when Toni asked me to write this article, I thought—no problem. Then I began to think—where are they? What happened to all that energy and commitment?

I attended a national conference of Black Lesbians and Gays in Los Angeles last February and was appalled to learn that in the opening session of the conference the only lesbian scheduled to speak was a woman doing a slide show. I listed to Black gay men tell, with a great deal of anger, of their battles with white gay men over who should control the pitiful allotment of AIDS funding.

I am buoyed by the knowledge that lesbians in the Bay Area are forming blood drives to give blood to AIDS patients; still I have to ask my gay brothers some questions. Instead of organizing and marching for people with AIDS or ARC, why not instead organize and march for a national health care system so that any person needing medical care can get it in this country? And if tomorrow I call for a march to raise funds to fight cancer—which is decimating my lesbian community—will the gay men be there?

I am saddened by the knowledge that the Pacific Center, which is a center for gay people which offers counseling, intern programs for future gay and lesbian counselors, and support groups, has been left en masse by the lesbian and third world staff, because the predominantly white gay male board of directors has not listened to them and has adopted policies and practices which threaten the existence of the organization.

So, where have we come since the March? Not nearly far enough. We are still fighting the same battles, because we have not studied our history enough to avoid making the same mistakes. We are still not demanding political integrity from our brothers and sisters and especially our lovers, and so we are still victims to those people who believe that "gay rights" means that they have the freedom to open businesses to exploit us just as much as their straight counterparts. We still have gay people who refuse to vote because "all politics is the same," while the neo-fascists continue to put amendments on the ballot in every election to reduce even further any rights gay people may have.

Yet, there is still hope. We have young gay people, like singer-songwriter Faith Nolan, who came and spent a day with me because she wanted to know what it was like before. We have young people who know that their ability to go to women's music festivals and bars was won by the struggles and deaths of people who came before, and who realize that if they do not pick up the mantle, all that has been won can be lost again.

"The 1987 March on Washington:
The Morning Rally" first appeared in *Hot Wire* in 1989.

# Two Plays
# Hard Time & Pinocle

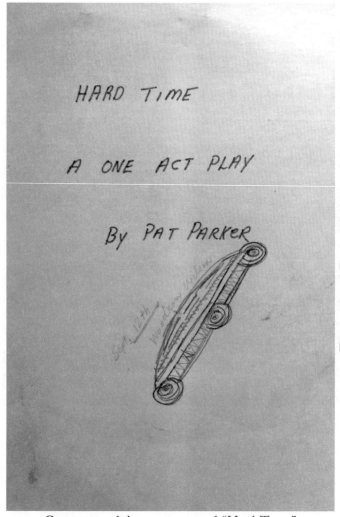

Cover page of the manuscript of "Hard Time."

# Hard Time

A One-Act Play

Characters (in order of appearance):

Officer Paul, a white police officer
Frank, a Black man in his early fifties, father of Uhuru
Uhuru, young black man, son of Frank and Helen
Richie, man in jail
Melvin, man in jail
Poppa, man in jail
Helen, Frank's wife and Uhuru's mother
James, man in his early twenties
Junior, the young Uhuru
Clifford, man in jail

*September 12th // Woodrow Wilson (text above image of a slanted vehicle or spaceship)*

*The stage has four small sets on it. Upstage right, there are jail cells. If possible, they should be elevated with stairs leading to them. Upstage left there is a soda fountain. A booth. Downstage right there is a small room. Down stage left there is a kitchen. The empty space formed by the sets should form a cross.*

*Setting: Interrogation room of a city prison. There is a large table with three chairs. An overhead lamp hands over the table.*

*Scene: A Black man in his early fifties or late forties sits at the table. He is wearing slacks, a shite shirt and a button down cardigan. His hair is cut short; he smokes a pipe. A uniformed white officer brings in a young Black man wearing flared levis, dark tee shirt, and Levi jacket. His hair is long, worn in afro style. He has a beard and moustache.*

**Officer:**   Here he is Frank. I'll be right outside.

**Frank:** Thanks, Paul. I appreciate this.

**Officer:** No problem, Frank. Sorry about your trouble. (*He leaves, closing door softly with great care*)

**Frank:** Sit down, boy. (*Young man remains standing*) Junior, sit down.

**Uhuru:** My name is Uhuru.

**Frank:** Well, whoever you are, sit down. (*Young man sits*). I asked permission to see you here instead of the regular visiting room. It's hard to talk to a person on a phone through glass. This way we can have more privacy. (*Young man picks at his nails, remains silent*) Why did you do it, son?

**Uhuru:** What?

**Frank:** Don't play games with me, boy! You're not locked up in this jail for playing jacks. You killed a policeman. There are four witnesses who positively identified you. Why son? Were you on dope or something?

**Uhuru:** I am Uhuru. I come from the earth to cleanse the earth. I killed a swine, a filth, a pig. It was stinking up the streets.

**Frank:** You sound like a Panther or something. Is that it? Did the Panthers put you up to this? Did they indoctrinate? We can get good psychiatrists to say they brainwashed you. That you didn't know what you what you were doing. We can get...

**Uhuru:** I knew. I am Uhuru.

**Frank:** You must be crazy. I have spent 18 years on the force. Everything you've ever had came from me and my job. I'm not a pig. I'm your father.

**Uhuru:**  I am Uhuru. I come from the earth.

**Frank:**  Dammit boy… (*He goes to the door and knocks*) Paul, get him out of here.

*The white officer opens the door and walks over to the young man. He takes him by the arm and leads him out. He is returned to the cell.*

*Setting: Jail cells. Two adjoining cells. In one, there are three men. One is about 35; the other two are in their early twenties. There is a toilet with no seat and a wash basin. Four bunks, two on each side. The second cell has one occupant. A young man. It contains the same fixtures as the first.*

*Scene: Uhuru is led past the first cell and into the second. He climbs into a top bunk, lays on his back, arms under his head.*

**Richie:**  Damn man, I'm hungry. Seem like I been hungry ever since I been here. Wish I had some of my old lady's cooking right now. Some greens and corn…

**Melvin:**  Aw, nigger hush. All you ever want to do is eat. You probably the only turkey in this joint that likes the food here.

**Richie:**  Well, it's better than nothing. I've had worse. Sides you gotta make do with what you have.

**Melvin:**  Yeah, make do. Nigger, you are pitiful. We sitting here facing all kind of time and you flapping your jaws about food.

**Richie:**  Well, what you want me to do? Ain't gonna do no good feeling sorry for myself. We got caught; I can't change that. Better to think about something good.

**Melvin:**  Well just tell me what is good about your old lady or her cooking. You know damn well that chick can't even boil eggs right.

**Richie:** Hey man, now you just cool out. You got no call to be rapping my old lady. She ain't the reason for us being here.

**Melvin:** The hell she ain't nigger. Who came to my place crying about money. If you hadn't...

**Richie:** Hold it man. Nobody forced you to do nothing. And for sure that liquor store didn't come to you. You act...

**Poppa:** Why don't you two knock it off. All the time fussing and fighting bout who's fault this is and that is. A man can't think for all your racket.

**Melvin:** (*winks at Richie and smiles*) You thinking about Poppa? You not thinking about that lil yellow gal are you?

**Poppa:** You best shut your mouth boy.

**Melvin:** Uhhhhh, whew! Hey Richie man. You hear Poppa. Poppa upset man. He got the blues. Thinking about his little yellow gal. Thinking bout all his hard time. Uhhh whew. I tell you man. Shore is cold.

**Poppa:** I done warned you.

**Richie:** Hey Melvin man, you better be cool. You know Poppa is a mean dude man. He a killer and don't take no stuff, man.

**Melvin:** Hey man, I know. Heehee. I'm over here trembling man. I don't want the cat coming down on me. He be done cut my throat or...

**Poppa:** (*moves toward Melvin*) Boy!

**Melvin:** Hey old man. Be cool! I ain't no young gal now. Don't be coming on like you bad or nothing. Cause I'll hurt you. Shit man, you better sit down and be straight.

**Poppa:** Then you leave me alone. I ain't done nothing to you.

**Richie:** Hey Poppa man. Don't get all upset. We was just joking a little. We didn't mean nothing, man.

**Poppa:** You two always making fun. You act like you the onliest two ever been busted for something. You ain't nothing. Holding up a liquor store. And couldn't even do that right. Hump. You two ain't so hot.

**Melvin:** Well at least we ain't in here behind some jive. You the one. At least we was trying to make some money. You in here on some chump shit. You ripped off a jive bitch. Hell nigger if the broad was wrong why didn't you just kick her ass or forget the bitch?

**Poppa:** Don't you be call Eula no names!

**Melvin:** Hey y'all. Let's be cool. Ain't no sense in getting all upset. We all sitting here in the same place, doing the same worrying about the same hard time.

**Poppa:** What you know? Huh. What you know about hard time. Ain't none of us got no hard time. That dude over there got hard time.

**Melvin:** What dude?

**Poppa:** The one they brought in last night.

**Richie:** Which dude, Poppa? What he here for?

**Poppa:** (*aware that all attention is on him*) Well, you remember the guy the policeman brought by here a little while ago? Well, him. Now the vine has it that he killed a policeman.

**Melvin:** No shit, man. He offed a pig. Wow. They gone do it to him. Shit man.

**Poppa:** And that ain't all. Story goes that his old man is a cop, too. A captain or something.

285

**Richie:** You jive, Poppa. A pig's kid. Naw man. That's bull.

**Poppa:** Naw! Naw. That's the gospel truth. One of the trustees told me. He was serving the guards and they was talking about it.

**Melvin:** Hey man. No why would they be talking about something like that with a prisoner around?

**Poppa:** Aw, come on boy. You know the white folks don't be paying no attention to us.

**Richie:** Well they shore enough paid enough attention to us. Wouldn't be here except for all that attention. Wish they'd pay some attention to feeding us better.

**Melvin:** Shit there he goes again. Always talking bout food.

*Lights go down on the cells. Comes up on the kitchen.*

*Setting: A small kitchen. Actually all that is needed is a table and chairs.*

*Scene: Two people are seated at the table. Frank and Helen, his wife. They are drinking coffee and eating toast.*

**Helen:** Are you sure you don't want more than that for breakfast? I could fix you some eggs or something. I'm feeling better now.

**Frank:** No, I'm alright. Haven't felt much like eating.

**Helen:** (Takes a handkerchief out; wipes her eyes) Oh, I know. Frank, what are we going to do? Our baby is locked up in that place. Frank, isn't there something?

**Frank:** Helen, don't. Junior is a man. And I don't know. He doesn't seem to want us to help him. When I tried to talk to him...

**Helen:** But, Frank, he's our son. Our only child. He's sick, Frank. He's confused. Junior would never hurt anyone.

**Frank:** Helen, stop it. Junior killed a man. A policeman. And he doesn't seem to regret it at all. He's calling himself some African name or something. He doesn't seem to care.

**Helen:** He's in shock. Something must have happened to him. He wouldn't just hurt someone. There must be something we can do...

**Frank:** Don't worry yourself, Helen. We can get him a good attorney. We'll probably have to put up the house in order to pay for him. Maybe they'll put Junior in an institution. He'll probably have to stay there a long time, but it's better than dying. You know killing a policeman is, well I don't know Helen. If he would just cooperate. Act like he's sorry. That policeman had a family, too. I mean, I'm ashamed every time I walk into the precinct. God, what they must think of me. My own son.

**Helen:** You can't blame yourself, dear. Nobody blames you. You're a good man. You've been a good policeman for almost 20 years. No one is going to blame you. They're your friends. They know you.

**Frank:** I know, but still. I just don't understand what happened. That boy had everything. A good home, clothes, school, friends, everything. I just don't understand. If he'd just talk to me. I tried, Helen. Honest, I tried. He just sat there and mumbled about being some African. I'll go and see him today, maybe he's had time to think.

**Helen:** Oh Frank, I want to see him. I want to talk to him. Can I come?

**Frank:** No, Helen. I don't think you should go. That place is no place for you. It's dirty, Helen. There's nothing there but losers.

**Helen:** Junior is there, Frank.

**Frank:**  I know but still you shouldn't come. Besides I'm not supposed to see him like I am. The guys at the station are just doing me a favor. Usually you have to go visit at a certain time and sit in glass cages. They could get in trouble if someone found out. It's better that you don't go see him just yet. I'll tell him you asked for him.

**Helen:**  Tell him I love him, Frank. Tell him I, well tell him...

**Frank:**  I know, dear – I'll tell him.

*Lights go down on kitchen.*

*Lights come up on soda fountain. One booth.*

*Scene: Two people sit in a booth. One is Uhuru. He is the same actor, but here he is younger. He is wearing a baseball cap and a multicolored tee shirt. The other person is a man in his early twenties.*

**James:**  That was a pretty big guy you were fighting there, little fella. Did he hurt you?

**Junior:**  Naw.

**James:**  What's your name?

**Junior:**  Junior Frank. Frank Junior

**James:**  Oh a junior, huh. I was a junior, too. My dad died, so I finally got rid of it. What was the fight about?

**Junior:**  Nothing. He's just mean.

**James:**  Nothing. You mean you got all those lumps for nothing.

**Junior:**  Well, he always picks on me. He doesn't like me cause my dad's a cop. None of them like me.

**James:**  Oh, I see. Kind of tough having a cop for a father huh. When I was a kid I always wanted to be a cop or a fireman something like that. Wanted my old man to be something like that, too. Seemed exciting.

**Junior:** You did? I don't know why? It's no fun. The other kids don't like you and you never get to go any place or do anything because your father's always working or sleeping. I don't want to be one.

**James:** What do you want to be?

**Junior:** Oh, I don't know. A pilot maybe. I'd like to fly planes. Sometimes I can just see myself flying a big plane, way up in the clouds. Nobody up there but me. Higher even than birds can fly, just me.

**James:** Well, who knows – maybe you will be a pilot. Hey, I hope you aren't upset with me stopping that fight. Seem like you both had enough.

**Junior:** No, I didn't really want to fight him. But he's been picking at me for a long time. My dad says a man has got to stand up for hisself.

**James:** Yeah, I guess he's right. I wish there were other ways to settle things. It always seems to come back to fighting someone or thing. Guess that's why we got wars.

**Junior:** Yeah, well, I gotta get going. My mom's going to be worried. Thanks for the soda. And for stopping the fight too I guess. I was getting kind of tired.

**James:** Hey, glad to help out. Listen, you know I'm not from here and I got no family around. Maybe sometimes you'd like to go to the park or zoo or maybe a ball game. That is if your dad is too busy to take you. Think you might like to do that? I live in the apartment right above here and I'm off every weekend.

**Junior:** Oh, yeah, I'd like that. Could we go to the airport sometime and watch the planes?

**James:** Sure, whatever you want. I got a roommate and he's a steward for airlines. Maybe he can get us aboard one of the planes for a tour.

**Junior:** Oh! Hey could he? I'd really like that. How about this Saturday? Could he?

**James:** Well, I don't know. I'll have to see. Anyway, we'll meet here next Saturday, say noon. And we'll go somewhere. It might take him a while on the plane thing.

**Junior:** Okay. I gotta go, but I'll be here Saturday and Thanks!

**James:** Sure, take care.

*Lights go on soda fountain; come up on kitchen.*

*Scene: Two people. Frank Junior and his mother. Frank is still a young boy. He is wearing a different colored shirt than in the soda fountain scene and the jail cell.*

**Junior:** (*upset*) I hate him.

**Helen:** Frank, don't speak that way about your father.

**Junior:** I hate him, ma. He had no reason. We're friends. Jimmy likes me. He takes me places. Dad had no right.

**Helen:** Junior you're too young to understand now. When you get older you'll see.

**Junior:** I see now. Dad beat him up, ma. He hit him over and over. And he arrested him. I see. He was jealous. Jimmy is my friend. He took me on a real airplane. And to the movies, and to the zoo. Dad never takes me... he's jealous cause I like Jimmy better than him. Jimmy didn't do anything wrong. Dad had no right to do that to him. He shouldn't of hit him.

**Helen:** (*Puts her arm around him*) Junior You're just too young to understand. That man Jimmy was not, well he's sick. It's not good for a boy your age to be around people like that. Your father was doing what was good for you. He didn't want anything to happen to you.

**Junior:** What could happen? Jimmy wouldn't hurt me. He's my friend.

**Helen:** You're too young to understand.

**Junior:** You always says that. I'm not too young. I know what I saw. Dad walked into the soda parlor and beat Jimmy up. He hit him and kicked him. And Jimmy didn't fight him back, He kept asking, "Why?" He didn't know who dad was. He didn't know he was my father.

**Helen:** Son, don't do this. You're being unfair. Wait, in time you'll understand.

**Junior:** You always say that. In time I'll understand. You're too young. Wait. Mom, you're just covering up for him again. Every time Dad does something you cover up for him. When he shot that man during the riot, you said the man was wrong. Well, Jimmy wasn't wrong. He hadn't done anything. Dad was wrong.

*Frank, Sr. comes into the kitchen. He is wearing his uniform.*

**Frank:** What's all the noise about? You can hear you two all the way in the streets.

**Junior:** Why did you do it? Why'd you hurt Jimmy?

**Frank:** Junior don't you know what he is? That scum was filthy. I don't ever want you around people like that again. You hear.

**Junior:** Jimmy was my friend and he didn't do nothing.

**Frank:** Now listen son, that Jimmy is a pervert. He preys on young boys like you. He should be killed.

**Junior:** Jimmy is my friend.

**Frank:** Boy, you're too young to understand. That man was sick. He should be locked up, kept away from children like you. He's queer.

**Junior:** Jimmy is my friend. He takes me places. He's my friend.

**Frank:** Did you go to his house?

**Junior:** Huh? His house. Yeah, I've been to his apartment. I met his roommate, Biff. He works for the airlines. He fixed it so we could go on this airplane and...

**Frank:** What did he do to you?

**Junior:** Do to me? He didn't do nothing to me. He's my friend.

**Frank:** Get your coat, Junior

**Junior:** Huh?

**Frank:** Get your coat, boy! (Junior leaves the kitchen)

**Helen:** What are you going to do, Frank? Where are you going?

**Frank:** I'm taking the boy down to the D.A.'s office. We're going to put that pervert away for a long time.

**Helen:** But, Frank, Junior says that the man didn't do anything to him.

**Frank:** But he was going to Helen, as sure as I'm standing here he had it planned in his sick, distorted brain. That man's got a rap sheet. He's been busted before for this sort of thing.

**Helen:** For molesting a child?

**Frank:** No not that yet, but for things in parks and bathrooms. He was building up to it. When I saw him and Jimmy last week, I knew what was going down. He was holding his hand. I know what was going down; and I'm really going to put an end to it. At least this pervert won't be walking the streets. After Jimmy tells what he knows; they'll lock this one up for a good while. I'll be back in a while.

**Helen:** But Frank, are you sure that...

**Frank:** Helen, I know what I'm doing. I make the decisions. This is for the best. We'll be back in a while. (*Frank leaves the kitchen. Helen sits at the table and shakes her head. Lights go down*).

*Lights up on the cells. The occupants of both cells are up in their bunks. The lights are dim. Uhuru's cellmate speaks.*

**Clifford:** Wow, I still can't believe that judge. That crap brain, decaying son of a bitch got some nerve. That dickless, punkish, honkey motha fucker. Hey man. Hey Uhuru. You cool, man. You got plenty balls. Why I thought I would die laughing at that cracker's face, when he dug you... I mean when you told him your name, man. I thought he would bust his gut. (Realizes that Uhuru is not responding) Well, anyway, man, you cool with me. You alright. (Turns over in his bunk)

**Melvin:** Poppa, you should have been in court today. I mean it was something pretty to see.

**Richie:** Yeah, Poppa. That dude over there is something else man. He ain't scared of nothing. He had that ofay upset.

**Melvin:** Yeah, he's down. That judge was rapping. Frank, something. And the cat says my name is Uhuru. (Gets up and starts acting out the roles) The judge, he say yo legal name is Frank something...

**Richie:** Simpson, man. Frank Simpson, Jr.

**Melvin:** Yeah, yeah right on and anyways the judge is saying, in this court, you are Frank and the dude cuts him off and says real low like, but everybody can hear, my name is Uhuru. I come from the earth. I'm here to clean it. And the judge is getting upset; he says Frank again, and this cat's beginning to turn red, dig. This is my court and I will not tolerate interruptions, and the dude interrupts him again and says, If you won't call me by my name, I won't listen to you and just turns around, Man.

**Poppa:** Naw.

**Richie:** Yeah, he just turns around; let's the dude look at his back.

**Melvin:** No shit, man! And the judge is upset. I knew ofays could turn red, man, but that cat must have turned 15 different shades of red. I thought I was gonna die laughing at that shit man. And the judge is screaming for the bailiffs to get the cat out of there man. He couldn't deal. He was beating his gavel telling folks to quit laughing and screaming at the bailiffs to get that cat out of his court. And we was cracking up so much in the prisoners' docket that he had them take us all back to the holding cells.

**Richie:** Yeah, that turkey was upset. He hollering contempt all over the place. It was something else, Poppa. You shoulda seen it.

*Lights dim on cells. Come up on interrogation room. Frank and his son are inside. The father is standing.*

**Frank:** Boy, have you lost your senses? What was that spectacle today in court? How do you expect us to help you if you act like that? Junior you can't act like that in court. Judges won't stand for that kind of stuff.

**Uhuru:** I am Uhuru. I come from the earth to cleanse the earth. I am the seed of the blood of my people. I am...

**Frank:** Don't play games with me. I'm your father. I'm not here as a cop. I want to help you. Don't you realize that? In spite of what's happened, I, we still love you. Your mother is sick with worry about you. I can't condone what you did. I can't understand what you did; I think you should be locked up forever, but it would really break your mother's heart, if you died in the gas chamber. She'd probably die with you. So you better start acting like you got some sense and let me help you. You know it is still a capital crime to kill a policeman. I don't know what the hell is...

**Uhuru:** How is your wife?

**Frank:** What? Oh, your mother. She's as well as can be expected. She's taking all this pretty hard. Had to get some sedation from the doctor. She just mopes around a lot now.

**Uhuru:** I'm sorry to hear that. Tell her not to worry anymore. Her son is dead. I'm just borrowing his body. I am Uhuru. She shouldn't worry about me. I am strong. I am from the earth.

**Frank:** What the hell's wrong with you? Are you nuts? You're no goddamn guru. You're Frank Simpson, Junior and I'm your father not some earth or blood. Are you ashamed of us, of me? People respect me; they...

**Uhuru:** Shit.

**Frank:** Wha...

**Uhuru:** Shit. That's what I said. Shit. Horse shit. Bullshit. Plain old crap. Respect! You don't know what the word means. Who respects you? Who? Your people don't respect you. You kill them, beat them, lock them in jails. And for what? For some rich ass white motherfucker that won't even give you the time of day. Respect shit, old man. You ain't worth a...

**Frank:** You don't know what you're talking about. People respect me. You think every prisoner in jail gets to visit their fathers in here? Naw, they make them sit apart from each other and talk on telephones. The decent people in this town respect me. The criminals and the malcontents don't respect the law, but...

**Uhuru:** What law! Are you the law? Yeah, you are the law. You with your gun and your club are the law. You're the law to your wife. You were the law to me and every other poor bastard who didn't have a goddamn thing or money to buy their way out. But what about your fellow pigs? Do you think they respect you? Do you? These ofay sons of bitches think you're a fool. A chump. A turkey. And you are. You've been on this force for years and what have you got? You should have been a detective years ago. And you had to fight your ass off just to get those jive sergeants' stripes. And the only reason you got those is cause brothers was blowing up stations and the white desk sergeants were getting killed and these bastards needed some Black cannon fodder. Respect! You're a fool. You've been killing your own blood and for what? Damn you, for what?

**Frank:** You're mixed up. I haven't been killing people. I've killed two men and they didn't give me a choice. They were breaking the law. They were stealing people's property. We need policemen. Somebody's got to do this job or we'd have chaos. Criminals would take over. The streets aren't safe, son. Somebody's got to protect...

**Uhuru:** Protect what? Protect the mayor from poor people demanding a right to live. Protect the governors and president from people wanting jobs and mothers not wanting their sons to die in fucked wars. Who the hell are you protecting? Are you protecting me? Yeah, you're protecting me. You've protected me from everything I ever wanted to do. The time you saw me holding Jimmy Fenner's hand, you protected me. You had that poor devil locked up and sent to prison as a sex offender; a child molester. You had that man sent to jail, and he never touched me. You made me lie. Great protector of right, you made me lie, and send a man to prison. And he never touched me. And you know what's so goddamn funny, dad. I wanted him to. I wanted him to love me. I needed for somebody to care for me, just as I was. And you made me betray him.

**Frank:** Son, you didn't understand. You were too young. That man was a homosexual. Maybe you hadn't been molested, but he was going to. He would have made you like him. Made you into a pervert hanging around restrooms and hiding out in bars. Feeling up little boys. That's not what I wanted my son to be.

**Uhuru:** What you wanted. That's what's wrong! It's always been what you wanted. Never what I wanted. Never what mother wanted. I never wanted to be what you wanted. I wanted to be me.

**Frank:** You're not being fair. We had some good times. Fishing, picnics, and what about the summer I coached little league. You were a hell of a ballplayer. I was so proud...

**Uhuru:** I hated it. Every damn minute of it. I never wanted to be a baseball player. I never liked fishing, but you couldn't understand that. No, not Frank Simpson's son. He had to be a man. A big, strong, virile man. A jock. You didn't care about me. Just what I looked like to the neighbors. You never gave a damn about my feelings. You're a man. Men don't cry. Men have to be strong. Have to stand up for their rights. Men have to take care of things; protect their families. Make a damn world.

**Frank:** But men do have to do those things. I know it's not easy. Many was the time when I wanted to do other things that I liked better. But I couldn't. I had you and your mother to think of.

**Uhuru:** But you could have done it, dad. You never asked us. You never once asked us how we felt about it. Mother would have done anything to... I guess she did. She sold her soul to you. And me. Did you ever even think about what she felt, her dreams, her fantasies? I never did. Now it's too late for me. But maybe it can be changed. Maybe some poor bastard won't have to live it like I did. Or you. Maybe some woman will stand up and scream; walk out. Maybe some kid will pick up that damn bat and hit his old man with it. In any case, it doesn't matter now. I've become what I wanted. I've become what I wanted. I'm strong now. I've protected my family.

**Frank:**  I don't understand. What are you saying?

**Uhuru:**  I'm a man now. I've protected my family from the criminals that would harm them. That's why I killed that pig. He's the criminal. You're the criminal. All the police and the mayors and governors that give them the orders, the right to do what they do. All the rich bastards that deny people their lives. The Rockefellers, and DuPonts, and Kennedys, and Carnegies. They're the criminals. Not the people you have locked up in this jail. They're free. And you and all the badges and guns and laws in the world will never be able to change that. I have nothing else to say to you. I'm ready to go back now and join my brothers.

**Frank:**  Junior, wait. We haven't talked about the doctors or getting you a good lawyer. We got to make plans. A defense.

**Uhuru:**  I am Uhuru. I come from the earth to cleanse the earth. I am the seed of the blood of my people. To the earth, I must return.

**Frank:**  What about your mother? Me?

**Uhuru:**  I am Uhuru. I come from the earth.

*The young man knocks on the door. He leaves with the policeman and returns to his cell. The old man remains seated. He looks at the empty chair. Lights down.*

Image originally appeared in *Pit Stop*

Pat Parker with her dog

# Pinochle

A One-Act Play

Cast:

Ann-Marie: a Black woman mid-thirties, casually dressed.
Lucille: a Black woman mid thirties, casually dressed.
Tish: a Black woman (thirties, casually dressed).

*Setting: The home of Lucille. Moderately furnished apartment. The scene takes place in her living room. It contains a couch, end table, and a stereo system, which rests on a shelf set. There are numerous books and stuffed animals. The radio is playing a local jazz station. In the center of her living room is a card table with four chairs. Two decks of cards, a pad, and a pencil are on the card table. A large bowl of potato chips and a small bowl containing dip sits on her coffee table.*

*Scene: Lucille is walking around her living room. She walks to the table and straightens the pad and pencil. She hums along to the music of the radio. The doorbell rings and she goes to the right of the stage to answer it. Off stage: voices.*

**Lucille:**   Hey girl, come on in. What'd you do? Buy out the store?

*(Tish enters carrying two large shopping bags containing beer and soda, cigarettes. She places the bag on the coffee table.)*

**Tish:**   Naw, I just wanted to make sure that I'm comfortable while I whups on you turkeys tonight. (*She rummages through one of the bags and takes out two decks of cards*) And I even got two new decks of cards. I'm tired of your old tired cards with talcum flying all over the place.

**Lucille:**   Well I thank you to know that I bought new cards for to-night. Just so you jive niggers ain't got <u>nothing</u> to bitch about tonight. And this morning on Starwise, John Wisser said that this is my night so you folks best getting ready for me. I intends to take all your money. Judy's is having their annual sale next month and I intend to get a whole new wardrobe at yall's expense.

**Tish:** Well, you just better slow down, cause if you're counting on my money for your clothes then you better see if Salvation Army is having a give-away. No way out of hell am I gonna let you take my hard earned bucks. Not today, no way.

**Lucille:** How's it going at the center anyway?

**Tish:** Girl, please. I don't even want to think about that place tonight. I tell you, if I wasn't a feminist, I'd kill some of those simple minded bitches that come through that place. I had some simple minded sucker cuss me out today, and I was trying to help her. Oh! I had to give this number to the service. I'm on call tonight.

**Lucille:** Why did the woman want to cuss you out, Tish? What you do to the child?

**Tish:** Me! Shit I did everything I could to help that dumb fool. I called hospitals all over hell and back to try and make things easy for her and she was too damn lazy or stupid to get off her butt and get to them. Girl, I had Labs in hospitals calling me up to find out why she hadn't showed. And this is after explaining to her, her mama and half her damn family why it was so important for her to go. Lucille, I tell the woman made me so mad. I mean ectopic pregnancy ain't something you just play around with like a damn cold or something. Anyway, I don't want to talk about that idiot or anybody like her. Where the hell is Ann-Marie and Theo at anyhow? This pinochle game ain't on CP time is it?

**Lucille:** Who knows. Ann-Marie has found herself a cute new number and it's hard for the child to get out of bed these days. And you know Theo ain't never been on time for anything in her life.

**Tish:** Who's Ann-Marie seeing? I didn't hear anything about this.

**Lucille:** Well, I wouldn't expect so. It just happened Thursday night.

**Tish:** Thursday! Two days ago Thursday. Where? Wait let me get a beer and sit down. This sounds like this is gonna be a tale to hear.

**Lucille:** Oh! Let me get this stuff in the fridge. I got some cold beer. I'll bring you one back. You hungry? You want something to eat, a sandwich or something?

**Tish:** Naw. Beer's just fine. I hit Flints after work today. They getting right funky with their ribs though. They must be killing some fat ass pigs these days.

**Lucille:** (Lucille leaves the room, off stage from the kitchen) You want a glass, Tish?

**Tish:** No thanks. I think I'll butch it up tonight. (Chuckles)

**Lucille:** (Returns to the living room carrying two cans of beer and a glass) Here. (Pours her beer into a glass) Yeah, Anne-Marie stopped by here Thursday and said she was tired of sleeping alone. Tried to talk me into going down to Ollies with her, but I was too tired to go off into a bar and especially that bar. Those ippy-dippy white girls get on my last nerve.

**Tish:** Come on now, Cille, you not gonna go into your Black nationalist bag are you?

**Lucille:** Not now. I'm not trying to put anybody down, but those folks in that bar bother me. I mean if you ain't a vegetarian, and have your whole horoscope memorized you can't have a conversation. I mean you can only talk about Plankton for so long. Unless of course, you're one of those Pacman freaks and I can't get into putting my money into a pinball machine so Ollie can get rich.

**Tish:** Yeah, but they got some sane people there. I've met some real interesting women there with some real consciousness.

**Lucille:** Yeah cause you fall off into your political bag. Feminist and communist and classism number. You can find a got damn flea to challenge to talk to. I ain't got time or interest in that.

**Tish:** Well, you better start taking time. Shit is gonna hit the fan soon.

**Lucille:** Yeah, yeah I know, but we not here to discuss politics. This is pinochle night remember? You plan on allowing pinochle after the revolution or is that going to be outlawed too?

**Tish:** Yeah, we going to have pinochle, but we not gonna let some no playing sucker like you play. Maybe we'll let you deal the damn cards.

**Lucille:** Hey, you getting pissed off at me?

**Tish:** Now I ain't pissed, but sometime I worry about you. You act like things are always gonna be the same. You'll always go to your job, and teach English and maybe in ten years you'll become principal and you'll always come home and listen to music and go out to a club once a month and fall in and out of love and it just ain't gonna be like that. These capitalist motherfuckers are getting ready for war and our asses is gonna be in a sling. It's not going to stay the same.

**Lucille:** Look Tish, I know that. I'm just not sure I buy your revolution theory. I can't see these people in this country revolutioning about nothing. Bloods want the latest rags and disco skates or some shit, and the white folks want to keep the bloods out of their life, and the Chicanos talking about getting land and I don't see all these people getting together around nothing but bitching.

**Tish:** But that <u>all</u> theory is a myth. It only took ten percent of the population to have the so-called American Revolution. It doesn't take <u>all</u> to do it.

**Lucille:** Yeah, but you can't even get women's groups together. How you figure to get women and men and Blacks and whites and Gays and Old folks and the working class and all those folks together. Shit. You can't even get the dyke's at Ollie's to get together around the music for the frigging juke box. I mean shit. I am not trying to stop you from doing what you think you got to do, but I just see a long ass road to hoe and a lot of pain and frustration. Who knows, maybe you're right; but I just don't know. And I'm not ready to take that shit on.

**Tish:** Cille, you ain't never heard me say a damn thing about easy. We're in the belly of the monster and he ain't dumb, but we got to try; otherwise we just lay back and let these bastards do us in. And remember, more and more countries are getting hip to the madness this country be doing. I mean look at Iran and Nicaragua and Chile.

**Lucille:** Yeah, look at them. Iran got some mad men over there and folks offing each other and Nicaragua is scared to death that Reagan is gonna kick they ass and I just don't know. Seems like you move two steps forward and three back. Well, we'll see. If anybody gonna make folks upset and revolt, Ronnie-baby will for sure.

**Tish:** Yeah, well he's definitely putting out some sturdy shit for people to smell. Anyway, tell me about Annie-May, excuse me, Ann-Marie.

**Lucille:** Girl, you better be careful. If she ever heard you call her that you would be in fist city.

**Tish:**   Hell that's what her mama named her.

**Lucille:**   Yeah, but you ain't her mama and she will get highly upset with your black ass for even daring to remind her of that. Miss thing would just as assume that East Monroe Louisiana never existed.

**Tish:**   Well that's for damn sure. She's almost as bad as this sister I met in L.A. who told me her name was Aynn Jo Nes and come to find out, her name was Ann Jones. I mean can you believe it. It pisses me off so much to think that those bastards got us so confused and fucked up that we don't even want to be who we really are. Damn what a crock of shit.

**Lucille:**   There you go again. Let me tell you about Ann-Marie. She goes down to Ollie's and plants herself on one of the bar stools. Now girl, you know Miss Thang was desperate. She probably ain't been on a stool in ten years, but it's harder to cruise from a table. So, anyway, she meets some strange white child. I mean this woman was a real space cadet. She starts telling Ann-Marie that she's from another planet, and we have to get in tune with the cosmic love of the universe. She says that she's not really a human, but a cosmic clone sent her to radiate tranquility among earthlings.

**Tish:**   Hold it Lucille! You got to be putting me on. No way in hell am I gonna believe this shit even in Ollie's. Cosmic my ass.

**Lucille:**   Naw, naw. I am not jiving. I swear on a whole stack of bibles. Ann-Marie said that she couldn't believe it was happening. She claims that she kept looking at the woman to see if she was stoned or something, but her eyes were clear and all she was drinking was that Crystal Geyser crap. Child, she had me in stitches. She said the woman claims that we have to release our souls and bodies to the universe. That we are throwing off the cosmic flow, because we deal in humanistic needs; things like love and jealousy are against the natural order of the universe. Animals were never meant to love; a bull doesn't love a cow. So sex is the end, the ultimate and we only serve to confuse and distort the universal flow by expecting anything but sex from our relationships.

Tish: Jesus H. Christ. Here the whole damn world is going to hell on a jet liner and this fool's talking cosmic. I can't believe that Ann-Marie sat up and let some turkey bend her ear like that and didn't say anything. I mean horny is one thing, but nobody is that damn desperate.

Lucille: No, she didn't go home with her. That was her first conversation. She claims that she finally told the woman that she was a demonic force set to destroy the world. That she ate the leavings of animals, heart, liver, lungs, that she practiced rituals every full moon to alter the course of the rides. Said she freaked the child out so much that she got up and left her crystal water and left the bar.

Tish: Well, when this new love of her life show up? And how did she have the stomach to talk to anybody after that first fool.

Lucille: Now, I hear that. She says she drank double shots for the next hour trying to get over that child. Anyway, she says she sitting there and getting more depressed by the minute. Some jive talking nerd slides in next to her and starts trying to make a play. Well Miss Thang ain't hardly ready for this. Says she's just about ready to cuss out this turkey, insult his mama and generally get quite colored and this fine looking young butch slides up and tells the dude, she doesn't appreciate him trying to hit on her old lady. Well, the dude apparently has had the ground rules laid out so he hats up and gets on down the bar apologizing the whole way.

Tish: God, that sounds like something Ann-Marie would eat up. I mean talk about old school role playing and romantic bull-shit. That chile is a born freak for it.

**Lucille:** Come on now. I remember when we were all working at the post office. You were off into the roles a taste yourself. You were supporting that artist girlfriend of yours and expecting your dinner on the table every night. So don't get too out there on Ann-Marie.

**Tish:** Lucille! That was in 1968! You know time does allow some people to grow and change. I mean then that was about all there was. Sides I never was really into the shit, but if I didn't half go along with the program, you all would have thought I was some kind of nut or something.

**Lucille:** Hell woman we still thought you was some kind of nut. In fact, there is some serious doubt about you now. (Laughs) You know you was just as much into the shit as everybody else.

**Tish:** Bull, Cille. I remember the first time I went to one of yall's house parties. I couldn't believe all those women walking around in evening gowns and tuxedos. I didn't know a damn thing about butch and femme. This woman asked me what was I and I told her I was a writer. She looked at me like I had lost all my good sense. Course once I found out that the femmes did all the housework, than I had no problem figuring out which one I was gonna be. Hell, I ain't never liked no housework. Anyways, you getting all off the track. Finish telling me about Ann-Marie's new thing.

**Lucille:** Yeah, she's this student from Berkeley. You know the type. Young, bout twenty-two or something. Athletic, nice body, wearing the latest clothes and just looking for a sugar mama like Ann. Definitely butch, into partying hardy.

**Tish:** Oh God. You'd think after Tony put that child through all the changes she did, that Ann-Marie wouldn't go near anybody under thirty again in life. I don't understand what she sees in these young idiots. All they want is her money, her taking care of them, cooking cleaning, wiping their puke when they drag in drunk after spending her money, using her car to chase all over Oakland. I don't get it. Young people bore the absolute shit out of me.

**Lucille:** Say what? I know this is the human loving person of all time talking this. This must be some kind of gist or something.

**Tish:** The word you looking for Miss smart-ass is ageist, which I am not, but I can't help making the statement. I mean the problem with young lovers is that I've already done most of the things that they are talking about doing and I have no desire to do them twice. You know what I mean?

**Lucille:** I must admit I know exactly what you're talking about. Remember when I used to go with Pam. Girlfriend, that child just about wore my ass out. Every night she was ready to go partying. And after eight, most times nine or ten hours a day trying to educate America's youth, I was not ready for party, party, party. Plus she'd get all excited about some jive like a women's conference and I couldn't get her to understand that after you've been to two or three of those things that they...

**Tish:** Two or three! One is enough.

**Lucille:** I heard that.

*(Doorbell rings. Lucille goes to the right of the stage to answer it. Voices heard off stage.)*

**Lucille:** Hey Ann-Marie. We were beginning to wonder if you were going to be able to get out of bed and join us.

**Ann-Marie:** Hell, girlfriend, I had my doubts for a minute there my damn self.

*(They enter arms around each other.)*

**Tish:** Hey, hey. I hear the little bird been hanging around your house, Ms. Jolivette.

**Ann:** Bird?

**Tish:** Yeah the bird of love or lust or whatever.

**Ann:** Shittt. Lust honey, definitely lust. But if this lust gets any better or hotter, I may just fall in LOVE!

**Tish:** Well, sit down and tell me all the de-tails, please.

**Lucille:** You want something to drink or eat, Ann-Marie?

**Ann:** Yeah, you got any pop? I am dehydrated something fierce.

*(Lucille goes off to the kitchen.)*

**Tish:** So, give me the scoop. Hear you found yourself a young Adonis.

**Ann:** Well, her name is...

**Lucille:** (*Walking back into the room*) Hold it, don't say a thang until I gets myself comfortable. I don't want to miss a word.

**Ann:** Okay. Give me that pop quick. I think I must have sweated off ten pounds in the last two days. If we hadn't planned this game I probably would have needed to be hospitalized for something by tonight.

*(Lucille gives her the soft drink and sits down)*

**Ann:** Well, like I was saying, her name is Theresa, but she likes to be called Terry. (*Lucille and Tish exchange knowing glances*) She's a graduate student at Cal in Social Work. She's tall and lean and a fucking machine. Ho Chile! She put some move to me that I ain't never seen. Um Umh Umh.

**Lucille:** So where is she now? Why didn't you bring her along?

**Ann:** So you old biddies can mess with her mind. No no. Naw seriously, I needed a break. I don't want to do a Tony repeat. Remember she came over one night and left two weeks later to go get her clothes and move in. No. NO. I plan to take this slow and easy, but yall got to know I haven't felt this good in a long long long time. That girl knows how to push every button I got. She even pushes some I didn't even know that I had. Umph.

**Tish:** Well, I'm glad to hear you haven't forgot Tony. I was worried you might be repeating history.

**Ann:** Forget Tony! Girl, sometimes I pray that I could forget that bitch. You know that woman had me ready to kill myself. Naw I ain't going to ever forget her. She made me have to take a long look at myself. I mean she left me with no money, no car, no house, no furniture and even worse, with no self respect. I thought I was going to lose my mind because of that bitch.

**Lucille:** Ann-Marie, damn. Why didn't you say something? Maybe we could have done something. I knew you were hurting, but I didn't realize it was that bad,

**Ann:** Hey what could you do? I didn't really want to be around anybody then. I needed that time alone to take a good look at my situation. And you know I didn't like every thing I saw, but I also figured out that I'm not such a bad person. I've got something to offer. And sides, I recovered most of my stuff. Couldn't recover that lost self respect for a while though. Anyway, enough of Tony. I wish the bitch all the hell in the world. You know if what they say is true about what goes around comes around then that poor chile is in for some really hard times. She might wake up dead some fine day.

**Tish:** Still, we could have offered some kind of moral support. I mean we thought you had everything under control. Or maybe we could have gone and personally kicked Tony's ass for you.

**Ann:** Not to worry darling. I did that myself. That's how I got my car and car keys back. You know the bitch had the nerve to make a second set of keys to my car for her sloosie. I bet she lost many points on the butch scale that night, cause I was on her ass like white on rice. Considering that yall didn't hear anything, she must have gone into hiding until she healed and took her lover with her. I didn't know I could be so badddd.

**Lucille:** Wait a minute. What do you mean you was bad? Are you sitting here telling us that you, Miss Ann-Marie Jolivette, the pride of the Alameda county Department of Social Services, allowed herself to engage in pugilistics? Naw, naw, I do not believe what my ears are reporting.

**Ann:** No, I didn't say a damn thing about pug ga shit. I went over to the bitch's house and kicked her long skinny ass until I got tired. And then threatened to kick her new cunt's ass too. Took my car and keys and told them both to stay very clear of me for a long time. And you know all the crap they tell us about vengeance is mine saith the Lord and forgiving? Well, let me go on record as saying that everytime I fired that slime up it felt sooooo good! I damn near had an orgasm from it. Got so stirred up I had to go to the bar and pick up somebody, all sweaty, bruised knuckles and all.

**Lucille:** If I had not heard this, I swear...

**Tish:** Chile, hush. You know in the same situation you would have been out with your little Saturday night special trying to shoot somebody.

**Cille:** Really now you know me better than that. First off, I would never be in that kind of situation.

**Ann:**   Wait just a mi…

**Lucille:**   Hold on now, Ann. Calm down. I'm not putting you down. The fact is you and I are real different when it comes to how we handle our lovers. You're much more generous than I am. (smiles at Tish) I'm too cautious to ever let a lover drive my car let alone let one have a key. Hey, if they ain't got they own, then they have to ride with me or BART it.

**Tish:**   Hey for real, the child is being truthful. I remember one time when uh, what's her name, you know the lab tech…

**Ann:**   Oh er Nadine.

**Tish:**   Yeah, Nadine borrows a buck from Cille so she can get across the Bay bridge and girl don't you know that Cille charged the girl a quarter interest.

**Lucille:**   Tish! You are such a liar.

**Tish:**   Naw really, in fact if the girl hadn't been in such a hurry to get to work, she probably would have asked her for collateral.

**Lucille:**   Tish you are so jive. Anyway, Ann tell me more about this new interest in your life.

**Ann:**   What's to say really. We're just getting to know each other and taking it slowly. Like I said, she a grad student in social work, which is nice, because I rap about work and she's really interested. The welfare department represents a career to her not just a temporary gig. She spent four years in the service so she's not dumb about what life is, you know. She's fun to be with right now. We have the greatest time in bed imaginable. Hey I got no complaints at this point in the game, but believe me I am going to take it real slow and easy. I have learned my lesson.

**Tish:** Speaking of lessons, when are we going to play cards and where the hell is Theo? I'm ready to start my classes.

**Ann:** Classes? Will you listen at this. Chum who do you think you selling? The way you bid over your head all we have to do is sit back and set your tail.

**Tish:** Well, hell as scared as you turkeys are about bidding, if I didn't open my mouth we'd play every damn hand at 50.

**Lucille:** Well, it's not our fault Tish, if you think being a radical means you got to be out in front in everything, even cards.

**Tish:** Wait...

**Lucille:** Hold on, I'm just kidding. Why don't we play a hand or two of cut throat until Theo gets here. She's probably off somewhere underneath her car.

**Ann:** Now that's for real. I do not understand why that chile doesn't buy herself a decent car. She's got money to afford it.

**Tish:** Hell Ann, if I were a mechanic, I would do exactly like she does. She knows how to fix them.

**Ann:** Yeah, but I'd at least start off with something that had a chance of running. I think she buys the worst wrecks at the dump. I think it's more of a challenge or something.

**Tish:** Well, the way this economy is going, we're all gonna be down at the dump yard pretty soon. You know the got damn medical department cut the lab fees in half last week. All our labs are calling and crying the blues about their bills now.

**Ann:** Well, of course we know. We have to make cuts somewhere; the states are being cut back by the federal government.

**Tish:** Lord, how could I forget that you are one of the chosen. Give me the cards, Cille and let's play. (Sits a the table, opens up the cards, and begins shuffling). You know Ann, the strangest thing about this new love affair of yours is that you stayed around in the bar after that cosmic freak...

**Ann:** How did you find out about that? Cille, damn you and your diarrhea of the mouth...

**Lucille:** Come on now, Ann, you know that has got to be the funniest story of the year.

**Ann:** Hell, you think that's weird, I didn't tell you about the one after that. This woman scared me to death.

**Tish:** Scared you, now that's hard to believe.

**Ann:** No, really. See, I called myself dressing to fit the bar, so I broke out in my Calvins and a cowboy shirt with a bandana around my neck, well that was a real mistake. This big ass dyke slides up next to me and says she's into fist too. So I looks at the child like she is strange which she was and says what?

**Tish:** You're not gonna say what I think you are going to say.

**Lucille:** What, what!

**Ann:** I kid you not. The fool was into that sadistic shit, and it seems that red handkerchiefs have something to do with fist fucking. I almost choked on my drink when I realized what the hell she was putting down. And girlfriend, that child was stone serious.

**Lucille:** Now you want to talk about some loosely wrapped people.

**Tish:** Shit, it's a lot fucking more than being loosely wrapped. Those conniving bitches make me want to murder. I mean to think that I and a lot more people like me worked our asses off for this got damn movement and assholes like that try and apply our work to some self-centered jive just makes me want to puke. Do you realize that there are some women out there who will seriously entertain the thought that they might be oppressing those women because they think the shit is sick. I just wish one of those bitches would approach me. Oh how I wish. The slimy dog better pray she a masochist, cause after I fire up her ass all she gonna have to enjoy for a long time is her pain. Jesus!

**Lucille:** Calm down, Tish. It's a wonder you don't have a damn ulcer or heart attack, the way you get riled.

**Tish:** Naw, Cille this shit is serious. These people are running around writing articles, publishing books, recruiting in bars and trying to pass themselves off as some kind of minority that's being oppressed.

**Ann:** Well, I tell you if the woman I met the other night is an example then they are oppressed... by a case of the uglies. (*They all laugh.*)

**Lucille:** Tish, are you going to hold those cards all night or are you planning to share with your friends?

**Ann:** While you deal, I'll get the drinks. Orders anyone?

**Tish:** Yeah, bring me a beer, please.

**Lucille:** Me too. No wait, do I want beer or...

**Ann:** I'm not a paid waitress; order now or get it yourself.

**Lucille:** Okay, a beer. Some people have no patience at all. (*Ann goes off to the kitchen. Tish offers the cards to Lucille to cut and then deals out three hands, five cards at a time and a kitty of five cards. Ann returns and they put together their hands.*)

**Ann:** Tish what kind of shit is this. You are one no dealing sucker.

**Lucille:** Amen to that.

**Tish:** Are yall really planning to start selling shit this early in the game? Damn!

**Ann:** Well, madam, I ain't hardly jiving and to prove my point, I'm going to politely (*Sits up very straight, purses her lips*) pass.

**Lucille:** Well, now let's see. If Ann is passing and looking at this mess, you must have dealt yourself all the cards, I wish I could run you up, but I'm not drunk enough to lie that much. Pass.

**Tish:** Oh naw. You jive time chums. Why the hell didn't you ask for a new deal? I would have given it up.

**Ann:** But it's so much more fun to set you.

**Tish:** You fuckers. Okay, I'll call spades as trump. (*Turns over the kitty.*) God dammit. I'm set. I needed a queen for a marriage. Okay, I called diamonds for the sake of your meld. (*throws her hand on the table*)

**Ann:** I've got 32 points thank you.

**Cille:** Shit, I still can't make the board.

**Ann:** (*Writes in the score.*) Minus fifty for Ms. Tish.

**Tish:** Bitch. That's alright this game is still very early and as some old white turkey said, I Shall Return.

**Lucille:** Yea well, don't forget what happened to that old white turkey. He got his ass fired for trying to kill off all those bloods.

**Ann:** Say what?

**Lucille:** Didn't your folks ever tell you why Truman fired MacArthur. Cause he was getting all the Black guys killed.

**Tish:** Girl, where did you get that shit?

**Lucille:** My parents. I remember them talking about it. They said Truman fired MacArthur cause he was sending the Black soldiers to the front. They thought Truman was God's second gift to the Black race.

**Ann:** Who was the first?

**Lucille:** Roosevelt of course.

**Tish:** I never heard that shit about MacArthur before. I don't think that's real.

**Lucille:** Why cause you didn't read about it in one of your history books?

**Tish:** Hey I'm no believer of history books, but usually you hear about this kind of stuff from another source.

**Lucille:** Now you got to know better than that. There's so much information regarding Black folks in this country that never see the inside of anybody's history book.

**Tish:** Yeah I know that, but usually you can find out about it from other sources. Leftist materials – places like the Afro-American Historical Society or the copies of old Black magazines or some place.

**Lucille:** Tish, you amaze me sometimes. Here you are, the Black revolutionary, and you are so willing to believe in "good." And rights and all that idealistic crap. Girl, how you going to survive a revolution? You believe in people too much.

**Tish:**    If you don't believe in people how the hell are you going to make it through life? I have to believe in people. That's what's going to make a difference. Hey, Che said it. The first love of a revolutionary is his people. I meet somebody talking revolution who's not talking out of love for people I don't want to know them. Ideology doesn't mean a thing without people. That's what rhetoric is. Deliver me from those kind of people.

**Ann:**    (*has been dealing the cards*) Excuse me, but are you two going to plot the political course of the country or play cards?

**Tish:**    (*they pick up cards and arrange hands*) No, but really Cille, I understand your point about our distorted history, but I'm just surprised that I never heard that thing about MacArthur.

**Ann:**    Yeah, I never heard that either, but I wouldn't doubt it in the least. It sounds par for the course.

**Tish**:    Yeah, well that's true. My brother used to complain cause he fought in World War II and all they let him do in the Navy was be a cook. I think the fool was lucky. Once they figured out that the niggers wasn't all going to turn tail and run, they put them dead in front of the guns. Look at Vietnam.

**Ann:**    Tish, how the hell did you have a brother old enough to fight in World War II? Were you even born then?

**Tish:**    Well, remember now I was born in '44 and was the baby of the family, and a menopause baby at that. My brother was the oldest, plus he got my folks to sign to get him in.

**Lucille:**    Why the hell did they do that?

**Tish:**    They found out the chump hadn't been going to school for a whole year. They figured that better he be in the service than in the streets. At least I should say my father figured; my mother wasn't too keen on the idea. And what my father decided was the law; my mother never heard of the Black matriarchy.

**Lucille:** Yeah, but in a war. Seems like the streets was a hell of a lot safer.

**Tish:** You don't know the Houston Police. They didn't believe in juvenile crime. They'd shoot a Black teenager, old man, baby. Anything that moved, they'd shoot.

**Ann:** From what I hear, they're not much different now.

**Tish:** Now, that's the truth. Hey, who's got the bid, here?

**Ann:** It's on Lucille.

**Lucille:** Oh I start with a light weight 50.

**Tish:** 51.

**Ann:** 52.

**Lucille:** Are you chumps trying to run me up? 53.

**Tish:** 54 – you're not the only person at this table with cards you know.

**Ann:** I say 55.

**Lucille:** 56.

**Tish:** Well, I lied enough for a while. I'll pass.

**Ann:** 56 huh. Is my card going to be in that kitty? If I bid 57 are you going to pass Cille. (Looks at Cille and flutters her eyelids)

**Lucille:** I believe it's time to get off the pot, Ms. Jolivette.

**Ann:**    Shit, I can't count on that damn kitty. Pass. What's Trump?

**Lucille:**  Spades, please.

**Ann:**    (*Turns over the kitty*) God Damn it! Look at this shit. My double run is in the fucking kitty. Damn it!

**Lucille:**  Well mine isn't. (*Picks up the kitty and puts it in her hand.*)

# Restored Poems

## From *Child of Myself*

# Assassination

It's Hunt's catsup
splattered over the country
like in some movie
and the dead guy
shifted ever so slightly
when a rock fell too close

but it is real -
this dead man
twitches in our minds
and we stop to scratch.

# Ice Cream Blues

here
        i am again
feelin good
feelin sad
        cause
they caught me
& swung
the blues
  down on me.

ice cream
        ice cream
vanilla and chocolate
child what you need
brown or white
        that
good good taste
make it all right

it was a bright pretty morning
when I rolled out of my sack
gonna go sell ice cream
then i'm rolling right back
here
        i am again
feelin good
feelin sad
        cause
they caught me
& swung
the blues
  down on me

ice cream
        ice cream

only 15 cents
little child with a dime
well you can have it for that
leavin a little kid out
ought to be some kind of crime

    ice cream
      ice cream
brown or white
good good taste
make it all right
went down to the job one day
boss man call me side and say
gonna have to cut you loose, my friend
cause you aint bringing in enough dividends.

ice cream
    ice cream
brown or white
that good good taste
make it all right.

# From *Pit Stop*

# To an Unlabelled

I'm playing a
game.
I don't know the rules.
& I should know,
that's why there are P.E. Majors?
But I'm playing
anyhow

The umpire or referee
or match maker said play.

& you

Jumped in the game.
unlabelled

So who are you.

Sister,
do I call you that.
I hope not.
Sisters are fat ladies
in church,
sweating away sins -
without rumpling their clothes
& keeping me in my place.

His wife - but,
you quit that game
back there,
you changed your uniform.
A regular on the squad

Concert pianist -
I don't know what that means.

I play drums.
but I fake it.

I think that's wrong - but
like I said I don't know the rules.

The game keeper is mad.

Friend?
I've heard that before.
It doesn't quite mean

I call you friend -

&

You know what I mean.

# Uncollected Poems: 1960s

# The Mirror

Gleaming pavements
stared back at me,
And talked to my
Feet as they carried
me to the rundown
Room where the
Fortune woman works.

I gave her the
dollar fee and
sat to know of
Tomorrow's tale.
Large emerald eyes
Looked at me
And returned
My dollar fee
plus three.

1964p

# Of Life

I thought if I were a sparrow,
I'd be free to fly and live;
I found out about the Hawk.
I thought if I were rich,
Things would be my way,
Then I learned of taxes.
I said if I were a man. . .
Then I learned.

1964p

I have seen death
Burst into a live body
& strangle out life
Like an irate husband.

I have seen death
Slip into a doubting mind
Persuade - Convince
the life - of death's peace.

I have seen death
Like a hard slavemaster
Command - & life ceased
From a tired soul.

I do not fear death.
I do not fear death.
I do not fear death.

1966p

# To a Friend
## for Betty Trope

I entered your fantasy,
Not a stranger, but
Not a friend.
I took a place,
once yours,
& claimed it mine.
You doubted but,
Did not protest,
for I entered
& claimed
as one close to your Sun.

You sat and permitted
my stars,
for love of your Sun,
& my form changed.
I became a Sun.
& you no longer a being,
watching stars,
but a new Sun,
in a new universe.

I beamed,
my rays stronger.
And yours,
lighting your fantasy,
making it real.
Your Sun becoming mine.
Mine                    yours;
Two universes become lighted,
Twice as well.

1965p

# City Song

Heat seeps from city pavement
Into, perspiring pores of Old
Auntie, sitting at her white-grey
window watching movement——
Wonders why she sits,
still.

Junk man father looks
at The team, and his
Family; telling his beer
of That. . . time when
He could of been a big
Star.

Young boy-man stands
on street corners with,
More boy-men talking of . .
Girls and enemy boys,
And week-end drunks,
And school - less days,
and THAT party THAT
Topped older parties,
And the next party
Which should be . . . . .
Better than all.

Project child in piss-reeked
Pants, panting after
Great chase of dirty
Bad men, Hoping . . . . .
That the latest
Uncle will give him
A quarter . . . . .tomorrow.

1965p

337

Child-woman remembers
soft words spoken
by her Man, while
Praying to the Unknown,
That her period comes
this month.

Weary woman walks
thru rat-ridden rooms
With precious remains
of this evening' supper
Given by her MISSUS;
Wishing it was time
to go...To work again.

City song sounds
from cracked pavements,
And airless alleys,
Unheard by heavy hearts,
Soft sounds - City song.

1965p

# Not a Good Night

"Do not go gentle into that good night"
    Dylan Thomas


I followed a path
        the path - it led
to somewhere. Curved
around space leading
me from my youth.
I met an old man.
"Old man, give back
my youth."
He gave me a gold pitcher
with a hole in it.

I followed a path.
        the path - it led
to marbles & jacks
& dolls, mother,
house, school, love.
I met a little girl.
"Little girl, give back
my youth."
She ran away
Her mother had told
her not to speak
to strangers.

I followed a path
        the path - it led
to a mirror.
I saw a face - not mine.
A face with lines
leading to pain & joy,
song and dances.
I wanted to dance again.

I skipped over guilt;
I laughed at failure.
I had never written a
"bad" poem.
For one moment,
I chased the lines away.
The lines crept back.
Crawling across my face,
the valleys and hills -
valleys of skin - no foliage.
"Mirror, give back
my youth."
The face in the mirror
turned away.

I followed a path
        the path - it led
to a river.
I bathe myself.
River, give back
my youth."
The river was muddy.

I followed a path
        the path - it led
to an unowned grave.
It did not say me,
Somehow I felt it was mine.

1965p

# To a Poet, dead

Swinging down a trail
             down a bumpy trail
  Hey,
watch the boulder on the right,
  (held by flour paste)
Skipping over rocks,
           over slipper rocks,
  (got no rubber soled shoes)
Run,
run down the trail, over the rocks,
to the path
  (a straight path)
fly high over that path,
to the temple.

Hit your knees
Oh, Zeus, Lenaeus, fair Muse
  & Jehovah too,
  I need you,
  you to me,
    for poems you see,
  Cause I wantta be
Poet

1965p

# Please you all

give me that "old time religion" or
        something like that.
& lo & behold
        a hand reaches through
stain glass window
    & you reach,
wine, red mountain wine,
wine like poets drink,
so drink,
drink deep,
drink long,
too long,
too deep,
& your mind sleeps,
& you are -
        a man drowned,
drowned,
    sinking down,
        sinking
                    down,
        spinning round                &
round
                    a top.
top can't stop
Sambo's tigers melted away.

1965p

# Two Faces of Black

I am a mistress to the Sun
I draw energy from its loins
The earth is my chambermaid
Its people are my slaves

Slave, your bones are tired
The sun is too hot
But your kids are hungry
You know you can't stop

I fly to the Summit of Olympus
Zeus is my houseboy
Pegasus is my packhorse
I am goddess of the Heavens

Fall on your knees woman
Pray to your new found God
Beg Forgiveness for Cain
Beg for a new face

The faces of Eve were three
I have only two
Time has made them strangers
One is only a dream

1965p

# Gold Stars & Hollow Bags

I

Gold stars given
for good work
in younger years -
Become meaning
of good things.
The search begins
to find
the biggest Gold star.

A Golden star
blazing - slashing
like a sharp knife
thru fog and mist.
Blasting out of a
black sky.

I'll be the Savior
when I get my star.

II

A hollow bag
Empty as death's eyes
Waits like a new grave
For a soul to become
its content.

Pliant bag
for the almost people
Sucks in life
like a dying man.

Bag people
Trying to get out,

to start their search.
It's hard to climb a bag.

**III.**

Star searchers
Run scared.
Bag's too close.

Star searcher,
Christ had his Judas.
Climb your altar.
Slash your throat.
Let your blood spread
like volcano lava.

Be a partner of death.
Grasp the star.
Hang on.
Clutch.
Then,
See if it matters.

1965p

A sea hawk soars above my head.
Circling, circling, teasing -
the sand.
Goes into a glide and lands.

Its fierceness vanishes in the sand.
Its walk - fast but deliberate.
No longer striking death fears -
A curious sea gull on the beach.

"It's different - little death & big death."
"I don't think so;
There's life after death."
The sea gull turns its head.

A beer can is popped.
The gulls scatter off.
Take to the sky - circling.
Sea hawks prowl above my head.

1965p

# CONFRONTATION

Stop !
don't you know what yield means?
yes officer
    it means

stop lean back

    let the other man

            but
my feet
    rebelled against me

would not move up or over to

stop                  for you

but i can not say that —

it's better

"i did not see you, officer".

1967p

# Berkeley '66
## for Bob

A quietness in this city

      lying stretched on spring grass

Motorcycle - scorched streets
    burned heretics of the past.

Blinding letters of neon stuttered words
 falling
   against my window like hail feathers.


bus STOP buy beach B A R gains brick
hut CREDIT cards antiques approved
black&white liquor mountains wheels
bodiespeopleflowers flowers pale

pale
            pale leaves rubbed in my hands

                oninto my pores

rushing
    a shower of sightstouchessmells

calm splashing over my body

     washing
         raining
            licking


a quietness in this city.

1966p

# A Voice from Watts

"God gave Noah the rainbow sign,
No more water, the fire next time!"

"Burn, baby, burn, — "

Black gods have called judgement,
give or burn, baby
    black god — a mad mother, him

spilling from ghetto stench,
    a mob,
    a mad mob without identity —
maybe a race that found theirs,
  & what you say in your white,
                Protestant, Anglo - Saxon
                    mother fuck the world church.
God don't like niggers —
    Okay —
           throw a little gasoline on
    Heaven
Gonna see if it burns too.

    Bring your troops back, big daddy —
need em here —
           cause Chief Parker ain't never beat
no Viet Cong's head.
           now you don't have to worry
about your woman getting raped,
               but
                  I really like to see how
peroxide burns.

1967p

# Poem to my Mother

Can you hear me?
I am crying
across invisible barriers.
They          are there.
My blood runs
down a lost trail—
My voice dies
against the walls.

I am crying—
I the infant
that suckled your breast
The breast — once full & ripe,
full of pride —
Now hanging limp
like a useless balloon.

I am crying—
I the child
that worshipped you,
for you were beautiful
& without fault.
No God could behold you.

I am crying—
I the youth
that doubted,
confused by suspicion.
You lied—
or made mistakes,
the difference — none
to the heart that raced
like a vehicle of my generation.

I am crying—
I the woman

separate & alien,
bound by visions—
visions too different,
different as our paths.

I am crying—
I want to meet you;
Your blood streams
through my veins.
I cannot deny you this,
your blood —
silent —
tells me nothing of you.

I am crying—
Your ancestors are mine.
Yet, our tongues
cannot form the same words.
Can you hear my tears?
Each weighted by innards.

I am crying—
I cry for the myth—
I wish for the snow
& fields that never were.

I am crying—
Must we be enemies?
I can not fight you.
Emotions make me a coward.
The conflict is not.
Is God so important?
Would He deny me you?

I am crying—
I want to believe.
I want to be,

the suckling babe,
the innocent child,
the youth — the woman.
I want to hear your blood—
to leap over the wall of time,
& claim you
& be claimed by you.
I am crying—
I am immersed
in a river of lost voices.
I am crying—
Can you hear me?

1967p

# Costume Party
## (for Gene Fowler)

Faces—
I have
        fallen in
someone's head/
laughter loud music
        smashes
          me thru
              bone
        cilia

  sweeps me

      OUT

faces/flesh

lovers tonight
to
      night
men's cries
Does bid their young,
      runon / faces
none knew me                 tonight
      I won the prize
              BEST
      masked/I came
              as myself.

1967p

Soldier's boots are
    falling
    shaking
    Whitman's ashes.

America has opened her legs
    a street walker
        to hate
        &
            the itches
      of her black pimps
          are knives.

Where is your hidden brook?
More important,
can I bathe in it?

1960s m

354

# With Love to Lyndon

"This is a sad time for all people. We have suffered a loss that can-
not be weighed."

Lyndon Johnson

I dreamed a nightmare,
This big-assed thing,
With a 10 gallon hat
& boots, stepped
& I was crushed.
My blood ran white,
Staining the floor.

I awoke;
& this hound,
without a hat,
or boots,
Not even a gun,
Wore a badge,
A red white blue badge
with big letters:
        OUR PRESIDENT.
& I wish he would
go back to his ranch.

You said: "This is a sad time,"
& I
thought you were talking about Kennedy.

I understand, Lyndon.
I really do sympathize.
You have a problem,
but, I didn't tell you to marry it.

I know this poet
He says we should love one another.

So, I love you
     love you
     love you
     love you.

Now, the next time,
you get mad,
maybe,
you should hit her.
It's cheaper than
shipping men to war.

1963 ? m

# white folks

don't think too much
about themselves

Always seem to be chasing
causes
"of poor oppressed folk"

like when the people
      of Montgomery
took to their streets —

next thing you know
half the south was covered
with white feet—

Used to sit and watch
white folks pay money
to be hollered at
sit & purr in their guilt
like contented cats

one day SNCC said,
clean up your own house
      go home
people's jaws got so tight
thought their mouths would foam.

Then there was
the panthers,
chicanos,
indians,
russian Jews,
vietnamese—
any oppressed hues

wonder when yall gonna start
unoppressing you—
yeah, white folks
    are definitely strange
running round healing
    other folks pains
hey — look at your homes
there's work to be done
you got pains of your own
a personal battle to be won.

 

1960s m

# Summer

It's summer in San Francisco.
The weather offers no hint,
but license plates flood the city.
Texas, Kansas, Michigan, Washington.
Tourist charge the cable cars.
An observant child shrieks,
"Look at the funny people, mommy."
A world wise mother sneers;
"Those are hippies baby."
My companion smiles at me,
but I'm not so sure.
His beard gleams in the sun.
His hair much longer than mine.
Christ had long hair.
In his day he was a savior.
Today, he's be a hippie
or maybe a queer.

Summer in Sanfrancisco
Marijuana bust in the Mission district.
An undercover man is a hero.
I ask my companion,
"How can you tell a copy?"
"They're big and tall."
But the draft cop on the corner
is only five feet - two.
I look at my companion.
Maybe he's a copy.
Paranoia Time in the city.
That's a good song title,
but they'd bust the composer,
Or send him before HUAC.
It's un-American to be paranoid.
There's nothing to be afraid of—
At least that's what the president says.

It's summertime.
There are more poets here
Than any other city in California.
I'm sure that's important.
But there are more baseball fans,
& baseball players make money.
Poets only make music.
Some people call it noise.

It's summertime.
The presido is beautiful at sunset.
The beach is crawling with swimsuits.
My roommate's dog shit on the rug.
But oh no — I didn't step in it.
My cat did.
Now it's on my bed.
You can't make love in catshit.

1965m

# From the Wars

Black soldier
Marched home
home to his woman
home to his boss man
home to his rack.
Hung up his balls

Black soldier
Turned in his gun
Should have kept it
Enemies not dead
Waited for him
with installment plan
& 20 - year mortgage
A broad smile
Pats for his back
a foot for his ass.

Black soldier
Can you speak
of a freedom
you've never had?
You're the nation's
greatest con man.
Why don't you
run for president?

1967p

# To a Deaf Poet

Your words tumbled out.
I listened, but could not hear
No,
      Heard, but could not understand.
And I felt guilty.

Your words stumbled out.
I tried to concentrate,
to change your song to my key.
I could not understand.
And I felt anger.

Anger, first at myself,
then you.
I said, "it was your fault".
I could not understand.

Your words stopped.
I had missed your song.
I wanted to say, "Let me
read your poem, please",
But I was ashamed.

1965m

Two people walk
into a park.

She carries a branch
torn from a tree,
caresses it
like a lover.

His hands hide
in the womb
of his pants.
He offers to
carry her branch.

Two people walk,
fade into the
night of the park.

I watch
passing unseen,
& wonder of
a raped tree.

1965m

Why burn a candle in daylight?
as the sun weaves like a needle
through clouds and fog.

my days are hued shades & changes —
among these,
darkness comes —
not dimming,
but casting nets before me.

For this, a candle
to eat nets;
to receive me through.

1966m

# Going to the bridge now

gonna jump off and drown
Going to the bridge now
Gonna jump off and drown
Cause my baby left me
Lord, she put me down.

Took her to a new bar
Prettiest dykes around
Took her to a new bar
Prettiest dykes around
When it was time to go
She could not be found

When I got to our house
she had packed up and gon'
When I got to our house
She had packed up and gon'
called up her mama
She hung up the phone.

I went down to her job
to ask her to come back
I went down to her job
to ask her to come back
Said she would not return
till niggers ain' Black.

Said I'd kill myself
if she's away from me
Said I'd kill myself
if she's away from me
Said she didn't care what
long as she was free.

1960s m

all

the sounds

    moving
swinging
       past

me
   & you

moving
   swinging

drift

in/out

fear not little children

sounds

beating a fast tempo

and
you

   and i

caught

dancing
   between the light

                  1960s m

the streets
    lying in union
with dark lovers.
    we, three
bearers of visions

        moving
        stopping
        moving,        across

            beds

street lights
    are ,
not torn
minds staring thru
    windows.

        they are,
that we may see
our touches
        magnified.

1960s m

There are so many bags to fall in
There's the pimp gliding down the street
the pig cruising down his beat
The fag beating some dude's meat
whole lot of bags to fall in

There's a lot of labels to pin on

Cock sucking uncle Tom
jive ass whore
bull shitting pork chop
& a whole lot more

I've seen a lot of faces
running down their cases—
people in many places

can't honestly say
i've met any body
in the same bag
in the same place
day after day after
      day

October 1969m

# Uncollected Poems: 1970s

# Speech by a Black Nationalist to a white Audience.

why you people
don't even know
what Black means.
I AM BLACK.
I AM SUPER BLACK!
I am Blacker than coal,
      Blacker than tar,
      Blacker than the
      Blackest Black,
you ever did see.

Why I'm so Black —
night time reflects off me

      and I hate you —

I am angry.
I am bad.
I am the angriest, evilest,
      baddest cat ever —

Why, I hate you so much that,
      when I holler

      HONKIE!
my teeth sends out Black Sparks.

yeah,
      I can't stand you—
Looking at you makes me sick.
In fact,
      the only reason I'm here
in your rotten presence,  is cause
your treasurer promised to pay me —
      with a BLACK check.

                     August 1970m

# Growing Up

a small boy
on a tricycle.
a 4 foot board
with a 1 ft.
board across
it's top
An intriguing
     T.
a small boy
on a tricycle
a 4 foot board
across his
knees.
resistance
to progress
a struggle.
a small boy
on a tricycle
a 4 foot board
hooked on
the foot
stand
 & great
progress.

1970m

# Fleshy Soft Sea

cold,
spreads
from my neck
across my back
muscles
become
warm—
a second of
no feeling
then sweaty fire
then swing

1970m

i will not always be with you

    even as i hold you
    trace strands of your hair,
i dance though mazes
search the end's light.

i will not always be with you
    as my mind journeys,
i return
    sometimes stronger —

caring even more.

August 1970m

not by chance
did our union begin.
no—
        a long wait

now moving in and out
        among silences

ah
        such explosions—

i am weak,
        but gain strength
— with each touch.

August 1970m

# Transit Lady

you move
into night, softly
like the touch of lovers
and
return
into a new day
smiling rose petals
—leave a question
answered by the gods
        or yourself
or both—
the same
leaving closed kisses
and a new day

1970s ? m

# A Woman's Love

I have sat in a lonely room
cluttered with words
of other's voices,
Making wall paper figures dance,
Dance for me,
Like jesters before
a queen's court.

I have lain
In our bed while,
you, love
Made word pictures
For other's eyes.

I have listened
As your keys clicked,
Snapped to your orders,
Like scared soldiers
In your private war.

I have hated your words,
The thousands of words.
Words in a citadel
I can never share.

I have hated your words
More than any woman;
Yet, loved your words,
Because they are yours.

1970s ? m

# "Good morning, Mrs. Parker. Are you interested in working?"

work

one can go for
long periods of time
without food.

...but    if your stomach
      is spoiled —

ladies and gentlemen!

      a spoiled stomach

stomach                you bastard

a hungry writer writes best.

                YES

poets should go hungry.

      my stomach

        is a poet.

a capitalist poet.

      Yes, I'm interested

            in working.

                1970s ? m

i have seen
    your hands
    old
    cracked with creation

i have seen
    you
    honest
    drawn with creation

i have seen
    you
    mold life from clay
    why?

why is it so hard
    to mold
    yourself

mold yourself
take your old—
    cracked
    clayed hands
& mold
    a free you
    mold out
    fears & doubts

Take cracked with clay senses
    & mold
    a creation
    an artistic creation—

mold, become
    a person of art,
    a free person.

early 1970s m

# To Lynda

Sometimes
i don't want
to be a butterfly -
& fly dipping,
off trees & things -

would be
a caterpillar,

    Wrapped
in a cocoon
    & you

are the threads.

early 1970s m

from my bedroom window
the city lights are calm
and i think of you


my fingers touch my body
& i wish it was you
here, tracing love over me


Even in my orgasm
my body screens
touch me, please


My screams won't reach
they lay here trapped
in the calm of city lights


early 1970s m

# Sunday Morning

Good morning
Garbage man
the sounds
of your labor
        jar
me from
 slumber.
you look tired —
        angry—

Does the clang
of the lid
 soothe
your mind?

Next week,
garbage Man
i will leave
 a flower
on the lid—
to muffle
the clash
 of metal.

August 1974m

# To Tamara (Tami) Kallen

Sister, we welcome you
our ranks are many
yet we are so few
within us
there is a place for you.

Sister, we welcome you
we will sing, dance & play
make joyful sounds
laugh and be happy
celebrate your womanhood today.

Sister, we welcome you
to help us share the pain;
to fight our enemies—
both outside and within;
to join us on our Freedom Road
in a tiring struggle with no end.

Sister, we welcome you
our ranks are many
yet we are so few
within us—
there is a place for you.

October 1974

# Gente

G is for girl,
where you at?
A common expression
to find out the facts.

E is for energy
which fully abounds
when this group moves
it don't fuck around.

N is for niggers, niggers,
all over the place.
It covers us all—
regardless of race.

T is for tactless
And this is a fact
If you jump foolish—
You'll be on your back.

E is for everywhere
Cause we continue to grow
Our isolated days are over
We'll have these no more.

And before very long,
& mark my words as true;
Folks gonna be chanting—
Me too — Me too — Me too

November 1975

# Cop took my hand

led me to his car
led me to his car
Say I'm busting you
for tearing up that bar

Drove me to jail
Shut me in real tight
Shut me in real tight
Lord, I'm so sorry
for getting in a fight.

Went to the judge
Slam his gavel down
Slam his gavel down
he says thirty days
for acting like a clown.

When I leave here
gonna make a trail
gonna make a trail
Keep away from bars
Keep the hell out of jails

March 1975

# Anatomy of a Pig

I'm a "negro" leader
I always try to please
Lined up at the man's slop feeder
Call me hoghead cheese

I am the black preacher
I humbly steal your MEAT
For Christ is my teacher
Call me pig feet

I am the intellectual
Kissing the man's cock
I'm clean cut & professional
Call me ham hock

I am the militant black
Telling the honkie to stop
I charge highly for my act
Call me pork chop

1976m

# [Limericks]

Left my home in Texas
Waved bye to my ma & pa.
Said, I'd come back someday
tho I tried my best
I never found the way—
ma & pa long been laid to rest

*

Met a guy in Indiana
From a rich family in Savannah
Wanted me in luridness with him
said he could make me rich
In two years without a bitch
but I couldn't stay & shake my traveling whims

*

On the road again
going through the country side
making friends
& leaving them behind—
Can't rest my head
till this traveling urge is dead
got to keep going & see what i can find.

*

Met this gal in Denver
She really care for me
Treated me really fine
She wanted me to stay with her
& tho i loved her true
I couldn't stay
cause i'm the traveling kind

\*

Now my head is getting gray—
and i got no place to stay
Cause I left everybody behind—
I hope on that day
when the Lord calls me home
There's plenty of space in heaven, for me to roam

1970s ? m

# Agua Riseuño

i looked that up
when i was supposed
to study —
learn about Mt. Eden
& i smiled
laughed with you
loved you
left you
 & went to Chino, Lake Mary.

Now i return
to listen to your
breathing
agua riseuño
so says Valasquez
& i took you
to the beach
of Santa Cruz
moved away to people
just you
the sand
the water
laughing
& i listened.

1970s ? m

# Poem #4 for Ann

i walk into your life
& ask you to come with me.
i'm not sure where we'll go
but i know it won't be easy.

i ask you to come with me
among people who won't understand.
They ask how can we love?
never why or how much.

i ask you to come with me
thru good time and bad
we will be crazy happy
hurt, pained and sad.

i ask you to come with me
among people of color
who will doubt us
and not trust me
who will say i fraternize
with you — the enemy.

i ask you to come with me
& we spend 10 hours in a boat
trying to catch fish for dinner
play pioneers of old

& we eat potatoes instead
giggle in front of the fire
feel good — cause there's no one
politicizing our feelings
just the night and stars.

i ask you to come with me
and we go into bars
& people say hello

& shake my hand
& smile at you
acknowledge you as the hand
i'm holding this month
& i want to scream
hey, this is my woman
but i don't
so no feminist will say—
i'm being sexist
& miss what i'm saying

i ask you to come with me
& we go to a supermarket
grin and dance inside
cause we bought a pot holder
and it's important
cause it's for our home
which to most is a raggedy barn
with independent stairs
going their own way.

i ask you to come with me
we walk down the streets
and i am afraid
of the bold one
who will say
what the others only look
& of what might happen.

i ask you to come with me
& we spend five hours
cleaning out a basement
& we sit on a broken couch
& you get a dirt mustache
combination Chaplin & Ronald Coleman
& we are two goddesses
surveying our creation
agreeing — Yes it is good.

i ask you to come with me
& we eat at other couples homes
& i think of my past fears
know how long and hard i ran
away from that label
blank and blank
& think now how proud i am
of the conjunction that binds us.

i ask you to come with me
into a world that grow smaller
people are defining the enemy
are defining away more people
day by day.

i ask you to come with me
into a future not known
uncertain, but surely difficult
i ask you to share your life
not knowing what will be
but knowing if we're together
it will be good.

1970s ? m

# Poem for Ann #5

Travel it is said
broadens your mind
refines ones senses

You and I traveled
covered the country
& I was afraid.

I feared our closeness
I feared our loneliness
I feared for our love.

Many poets have traveled
Gone the route I went
Know the pressure.

I was advantaged
Possessed more than they
I had you.

Travel it is said
broadens your mind
refines one's senses.

My mind has been broaden
I see another part of you
Another part for me to love.

June 1975

i must learn
again
to laugh
to sleep with you
Now i can only
watch
you breathe dreams.

1970s ? m

Lady,
rise from my darkness
fresh —
a virgin plum
safe
come open —
come warm to me
come like words —
        printed on paper
ordered —  spaced
come tangled —
        weeds and flowers
come to me blank
& i will hear
        i will learn
        i will,
                myself to you —
                        to know
                        to see
                        to be
                myself & you
Lady —

        hello.

1970s ? m

# well, i got the menstrual blues

chorus:
i got the menstrual blues
my baby's on her period
won't let me love her,
till she's through.

i remember it was many years ago
first time i saw the menstrual flow
ran home to my mama—
say Lordy what's this
said baby that means that now you're a young Miss

came out a few years ago
gay life is so good—
won't ever let it go
loving 2 weeks a month
ain't so fine
but can't be helped, unless
her period comes with mine

talked with my friend
said, girl i'm so sad
menstruation periods gonna drive me mad
She said, Fool & slammed down her cup.
What's wrong with you—
don't you like to eat ketchup?

now i'm feeling good
in fact, just fine.
me & my baby make love all the time
it don't matter
time of month,
night or day
I owe all my thanks
to Tampax and Tassaway.

1970s ? m

# my baby's a bass player

fingers me all the time
my baby's a bass player
fingers me all the time
& when she get down
 makes me feel so fine.

she plays her modes, everyday
from A to A makes me say
Jesus honey your hands so kind
Don't think i'll last
till you start on your lines

She studies chord changes day & night
practices charts until they're just right
But what really makes my temperature rise—
is when she gets down on me
and starts to improvise

She plays her notes for hours at a time
the utility bill here is some kind of crime
every time she touches me
i let out a scream
Thank you, Jesus
she don't play the tambourine

1970s ? m

I fell in love some time ago
with a woman who's very bright
she teaches school
plays by the rules
comes see me late at night
I can't help but wonder
when you kiss & hold me tight
Is your closet door a squeaking
as you're slipping out at night

She says it's just a short time
Her tenure almost here
No chance to lose her teaching seat
We can walk down the streets
No colleagues to be feared
I can't help but wonder
when you kiss & hold me tight
Is your closet door a squeaking
as you're slipping out at night

I'm hoping that the time has come
To set the straight world right
Lies & deception put to end
let the world know we're more than friends
And we can step into the light
I can't help but wonder
when you kiss & hold me tight
Is your closet door a squeaking
as you're slipping out at night

1970s ? m

# A Walk

Down this street
the wrong way
bounce off
evening rush faces

Past trees fucking
in the wind
Past people
in the wind

Up this street
to the school

"Hey is that
a boy or a girl
It looks like a boy
but. . .

no boys
no girls

only energy

flashing back
and forth
a joke of
some body
more roles
to confuse
simple-minded
folk
& watch out
even more
for adolescence
myths &

adult
     hood
  or
head
     trips

it is all a trap

beware of mother's cookies, children

Across this street

now
    my toes are tired

27.5 organisms
per city block

It is almost

too much —

 walking

1970s ? m

She comes to me — tentative
not sure
the ghost of past love
Dance around my bed

Are you ready now
for me? — she asks
your wounds are wide
& tender to the touch—

Woman — I have crossed
Hell — carrying
rejection and hatred
now — I am thirsty.
Come to me
I want to drink your juices.

1970s ? m

# Sister

Is your head on right?
Are you just uptight
Do you really want to fight
Child—is your head on right

1970s ? m

Every once in a while
I think I [am] losing my mind
going mad with madness—
going insane—blowing
my brain—

When I was a child
It seemed simple & plain
There was good & bad
Right and wrong—
Fair & unjust—

I read in the paper
that there's a
revolution brewing
in a country called Iran

1979 m

# Does This Make Sense

I used to think that
logic & reason prevailed—
Fair & just were clear
to see
Right and wrong a given—
But now—I read the papers—
watch the tube
& come away from both
doughtful and confused—
"Headline"
Families in the East Bay
under attack—
Some erratic drivers
drive a car into a Black
families house—
Burn crosses in their yards—
Throw stones through their windows—
Police investigate
Some of the culprits
are found—
But released—
Juveniles—they say—
Children's pranks—
no bigotry here—

1970s ? m

At first, I
dismissed the notion
tossed it like highway
litter, not casually
for penalties do exist—
yet old messages
burglarized my
thoughts
"History does repeat itself"
I am appalled—
the jowls of
Richard Milhous
have been replaced
by the specter smile
of Ronald R—
The riots on the east
coast moved further south—
Blacks, again in protest
Another body felled by policeman judges
people without jobs multiply
faster than roaches
Social programs fall like
summer hair beneath
the barber's shears
I am anger
wait—
I am not Humphrey Bogart
in Casablanca
No—Sam—let's not
hear it again or do it
it again with Bill Cosby
Let's not—
But the might makers ignore
me—

We are doing it again
slight alterations in
the scenario—
The "Mod Squad" becomes
the "Renegades," but we
go on with the same song
I am prophetic—
Hear me—

Last time around
the nation chose to follow
the moderate path—
Marched with Martin
while Malcolm stood
laughing in a corner
at the haste with
which we fled
down the path

Don't expect the words
of Martin to be heeded
again—It['s] difficult
to understand them
muffled by dirt and
tombstone

1970s ? m

# Just Exactly What Is It That You Want

I've heard that—
My mother asked—
When I said no—
I will not be a teacher—
Improve the minds of
southern youth
And buy a house on Sugar Hill—

Just What Exactly Is It
That You Want—

I heard that
My husband asked
when I said No—
I will not be the Black
Bohemian writer's wife
will not serve burgundy wine
and discuss Richard Wright

Just Exactly What Is It
That You Want—

I heard that
when I said no
I will not be
the liberal white executive's wife
will not serve martinis
and
take walks in the
Berkeley Hills

Just Exactly What Is It
That You Want

I heard that
when I said no
I will not be the
bed hopping poet
claiming "relationships"
that burn out faster
than ignited gasoline

1970s ? m

# Uncollected Poems:
# 1980s

I have a lover
who is strong—
Does not jump when I holler
Does not take all my words
as edicts from God—

I have a lover
who is loving—
holds me when I am tired—
Rubs me when I am tight with anger—

I have a lover
who understands
Does not think me crazy
when I share my dreams
Does not think me foolish
when I am the fool

I have two daughters
who think of me
not as the poet
not as the businesswoman
only as mama
and that is exactly what I want

"I'm so tired of hearing
about oppression"
Woman at Poetry Reading

Once it was said—
We only need to tell people
Show them the facts—
& they will become a mighty force
hear so common head
& move the madness away
and it seemed so.

Thousands of bodies
took to southern streets
a shield
Rendered fire hoses dry
Defanged the dogs
Turn club into straw
The people were told
The people were shown
They became a mighty force
& turned the south around

Thousands of bodies
took to the country's streets
A Rage
Bombers stopped flying
Soldiers stopped warring
Hawks were eaten by doves
The people were told
The people were shown
A war passed into history—

This it seems—
Is all that is needed—

Simply let
the people know—

A new species surfaces
They have no ears—
They had no vision—
They watch the actor
in the white house
& believe it's a movie—
Pay the price of admission—
See the play
then go home—
Yet the play continues—
Poverty still blankets
too many homes
the cast is more colorful
the sexes are shifting
Wars still smolders
The players have changed colors
The curtain will not fall

Oh sister,
my dear sister
safe in Nebraska flatlands
secluded in ivory towers
Think for one minute
If you in this decade
are so tired of
hearing about oppression:
How tired are we
of living in it.

# I'm Still Waiting To Be Pinched

Have you ever felt
You were in a dream
& needed to be awaken,
but you were already awake?

# For Wayne

FAGGOT!
Not me

gay
homosexual
faggot — no
how does the word
this metaphor become
men
tossed at the feet of witches
ignited
fuel for flames
flames
to destroy the different ones
the men were different too
they walked with women
walked as friends
never lovers
they walked with women
embraced them
supported them
believed in their magic
they died with them
faggot flesh to fuel flames
flames for witches
flames for strong women
flames for the different ones
FAGGOT
an honorable word
only suited for men
men who dare
only suited for men
men who stand with their sisters
only suited for men
men who are brave
brave enough

to blast the closet door
brave enough to say
I love this man
and all men
only suited of men
men who face death
the death
that walks the streets of this city
that comes with the faces of babies
that turns flesh to flame

Oh yes my brother —
you are a faggot.

# I hear a train a coming

moving down the track
I hear a train a coming
moving down the track
I hear a train a coming
moving down the line
O Lord, let it please
be bringing my baby back

it's been a long time
since she went away
it's been a long time
since she said good-bye
It's been a long time
since she walked out the door
Lord, I can't take
this loneliness any more

It's been a long time
since we had that fight
It's been a long time
since she cried all night
It's been a long time
since those angry words were said
I can't stand no more
of a cold & empty bed.

# Reflections on a March

### I.

Sometimes,
I feel I'm in a time warp—
I listen—people speak
& I look to see what year is it.

Washington D.C. Nov 11, 1987
750,000 people
if you believe the march organizers
650,000
if you believe the District of Columbia police
200,000
If you read the Tribune
Hundred & hundreds of bodies
March thru the streets
And I can help but wonder—
How many would march in their hometown.

I remember a conversation
with a woman on my softball team.
"My mother's coming—
I'm sure she knows I'm gay.
I tell her if she ask."
I tell her if she asks
I tell her if she ask—
I've had this conversation—before
so many times
so many years

### II.

I remember another march
Hundred & hundreds of people
singing "We shall overcome"
saying—no more chains—
slavery is over—

& I go out to dinner
with a young Black woman
She wears a studded leather
collar around her neck
Her "Master" is a white
woman from Maryland
born & bred—
& the only difference
I can see—
is that the sister
put the collar on her neck

III.

People magazine says
Moms Mabley was a dyke
Would Moms have marched
that day—
or any day
Did she walk those miles
in her mind—
or would she still
sit on stage &
tell of old men who can't
& young men who won't.

IV.

Hundreds of thousands
of people march thru the streets
then go home—
& I wonder how much longer—
how much more time—
Sometimes,
it seems we
need oppressors—
we take the keys
& lock the doors
ourselves.

# Sweet Sweet Jimmy

Your words are razors
cutting through coke
swift, grinding
and the world listens

The sharpness of your anger
frightens—they scuttle
to contain you—
The new Richard Wright
and the anger rises

Sweet Sweet Prince Jimmy
Are you resting well?
Does sleep cool the rage?

# Sweet Sweet Prince Jimmy

Sweet, sweet prince Jimmy
Are you resting well?
Has the anger gone its way?
Has the rage dispelled?

He was a funny looking
bugged-eyed faggot
and that
made the world angry

His words were like razor
blades cutting cocaine—
sliding the lines of trues
into sections to be
inhaled into one's soul

He warned of ignorance & hatred
consuming us all—
a mighty python cracking our bones
& swallowing us—
And we listen—then turned away.

# The Long Lost Ones

no   no   noooo
the whispers whip
around your lives
like a mighty python
choking the soul out.

Hide it, hide it, hide it
Keep it locked tight
Can't let them know you're queer
Keep the closet door shut by fear.

It takes so much energy to live a lie,
One's soul sapped by secrets.

# To My Straight Sister

"It's against my religion to read poetry with a lesbian."
"I don't mind reading the poem as long as she doesn't make a pass
at me."
                              Two Ohio women.


Soooooooo,
you think I want your body.
Plan to throw you down
on this auditorium floor
and
CONVERT you

or wisk you away
on my Harley-Davidson
to my hotel room
perhaps
ply you with wine
rip off your clothes
and
Take you

Take you in that secret way
that only lesbians know
make you a prisoner of my tongue
and a slave to my mind
and Ruin you

Your Jesus sits on his throne
waits to mark against you
your nearness to me.

Sister,
have you picked your stone?
Are you really ready
to cast it against me?

Perhaps you should know
I like my women strong
not fearful of the unknown
able to walk ways
not travelled before
able to bend in strong winds
not snap like dry kinder

Gay people call heterosexuals

STRAIGHT

like straight and narrow
or
in other words, rigid

Perhaps my sister
there is a fantasy here
of lust and loins
of ravenous seductions

but,

I know it's not mine

so it must be yours.

# Words

Riding in from the airport
She says "my partner"
I say "my lover"
Neither word seems right
Partner brings pictures
of offices and desk
going to bank
having policy meetings
lover brings images
of sweating bodies
and tousled sheets
smells of sex
wife? no
that brings pictures
of husbands—
& a wife—I'll never be
significant other?
but that's not enough
when I opened my eyes
after surgery and saw your face
you were not an other
when you bathe me
because I couldn't raise
my arm above shoulder
you were not an other
when you told me
I was beautiful
and desirable
you were not an other
when you held me
as I talked of death
and the world still undone
you were not an other
you were
my one true love
my one
my significant one.

# Oprah Winfrey

sisters talking
bout this sister
so I taped her show
sat down on a Saturday
to check her out.
now THIS is
a fine looking sister
solid looks like she
take on a n y b o d y
      yet      soft
flowing scarfs
and a light hand
that reaches out
to rub a shoulder
or pat a back
My initial impression
was definitely good
and I watched
Ms. Oprah work.

She talks with children
seduced into static cults
and their mothers    who
still couldn't believe
what happened and how —
their faces sad
as their children
tell of drinking blood
and animal sacrifices

she listened intently
as ex-satanist told
of rituals and hinted
of human sacrifices
but couldn't really

say because of
possible prosecution
and I was surprised —

Next she took
the Klan
and I had to admire
her self-restrain
couldn't see me
in a room full of hatred
and not lashing out
and I was spent —

Had to leave Oprah
and come back later
and sister Love was
talking to rapists
men who calmly sat and
told of abuse molestation
even murder
told of thousands of children and women

Oprah was cool
a barrier
between her guest
and the room
the women with no love.

And then the very next show
she brought out
the rapists' wives
the women who
stood by their men
including one woman
who stood by her man
even though he raped
her daughter —

Now
I have to give
credit to Ms Winfrey
she definitely be
an amazing sister
she be wheeling and dealing
with all sorts of folks
and I have just one
question —

after watching weeks of her shows
how come?
or rather who?
where?
do folks in this
country get off
calling gay people
   Queers.

I remember—
so many lives ago
when I was a child
I saw a picture, in the Houston Informer
of a man—
a young Black man
hanging from a tree.

I remember being shocked—
not at his hanging
rumors of such things
were known to me
but he had hair
on his chest—
no shoes or shirt
& I remember
staring at his chest—
I had never seen
a Black man with
hair on his chest.

I've since dreamed
about him—
his face—slack
no echo of life in him
yet so peaceful—

One would think him
just asleep—
were it not for the tree
and the rope

I rarely dream of him, now
yet
his image still hovers—

When I read about
Timothy Lee—
his image appeared—
not the smiling young
man with large eyes
the hairy chested
man with no
echo of life.

When I read about
Jacqueline Peters—
he appeared again—
his chest still hairy
his face still slack.

But wore a dress
a wide-brimmed
hat—head cocked
to one side—

And I stare at these
faces from the Contra Costa Times
and wait for someone
to wake me up.

# Timothy Lee

he, he, he,
Timothy Lee,
he, he, he
swinging from a tree
he, he, he

police say suicide
family say racism
friends say homophobia

one thing certain

Timothy Lee is dead
Found hanging from a tree
in the Concord Bart station

Timothy Lee
he, he, he
Swinging from a tree
he, he, he,

One California night
not Texas, not Georgia
He made a phone call
said, "I need a ride"

no one came
      or
someone came

Timothy never came home
He swung dark and heavy
in the California night
no light in his eyes
no life

Some say he took his life
no heart left
tired of himself
turned the switch – off

Some say the racist did it
Caught a nigger alone
isolated in the night
and took his life

Some say the homophobics
saw a faggot
saved the world from AIDS
and took his life

Timothy Lee

he, he, he
Swinging from a tree
he, he, he,

the mystery remains

In the 1980's

men still die
because they're Black

men still die
because they're gay

men still kill themselves
for both reasons

Timothy Lee is dead

the sad part
the mind troubling part
the can't sleep well part

is that at this point

in these times

no one can say

for certain

    why

Timothy Lee is dead.

little Billy Tipton
tiptoed thru his life
found himself a woman
took her for his wife

played his music
formed his own band
Oh my goodness!
Billy Tipton ain't a man.

Billy Tipton was a lie
covered in deceit
teeming in fear
hidden deep deep deep
behind closet doors

it's difficult to imagine,
yet so easy to know
how a woman can hide herself
for her entire adult life.

Billy hid herself
as my mother hid herself
as I have hidden myself
as women have
always hidden themselves
as I vow to change this world
so my daughters will never
have to live in shadows.

The closet is a lonely place
a tomb of self-hatred
that daily chips away
our ability to bear light

and we become modern day vampires
fearful of the sun.

I cry for Billy Tipton
she never knew
her lover's touch
the soothing words
to desolve cramps
the deep kneading
of a lover's fingers
to push away
the knots gathered
during the day.

I cry for Billy Tipton
she never knew the joy
of her body being bathed
the anticipation and lust
in a shower on a hot day
the tingling jolt of a pat
on your butt as you walk by
the rush of your body
as you give yourself to your lover.

I cry for Billy Tipton
She never held her children
to her breast
lay them clean and powdered
across her stomach
held their hands as
they kicked across a pool.

I cry for Billy Tipton
I cry for Billy Tipton
I cry for Billy Tipton

cause she never knew
how good it feels to

stand in front of a mirror
to look at her woman's body

I cry for Billy Tipton
cause she never knew
how good it feels
to be a woman

I cry for Billy Tipton
cause she never knew
how good it feels
to be a woman
who loves women

and not give a damn
what anybody thinks.

We're the Dunham-Parker's from Pleasant Hill
We're here to tell you what we really feel

What this whole gig is really for,
is to sing the praises of Hal & Elinor
Git down—git down

So raise your glasses; sing out your cheers
they've been in love for 50 years

We can learn a lot from these two
They'll show you how to make a marriage do
They got class
They got grace
They got kids
& grandkids
all over the place
But most of all
They got love—
love for each other
love for the clan
love for their God
love for Everyman
So now we'll split this scene
and all we ask
is that your anniversary
be an out of sight blast

It's not so bad
when your life is
enclosed in parenthesis,
born,          died,
definite & final.

It's not so bad
when the unknown
becomes known.
cause of death, and
time are projected
on scales and graphs
like tide flows

It's not so bad
when friends as
"How are you?" and
you see their bodies
tense – buffer
for your answer

It's not so bad
as the distance
l e n g t h e n s
clear walls build
between you and
the healthy ones.

what really hurts,
causes heart aches
and silent screams
is to watch people
    prepare
for your death
and you haven't.

"What makes you have cancer? Who gave it to you?"
Anastasia Jean

There are those
some new thinking
enlightened ones
who say—
illness is desired
brought on by the will
of those of all—
they say—
we chose our deaths—
instruct our bodies to cease.

I grew up in the American south—
heard the world nigger at 5
was first told I was no good at 6
saw police beat a Black man at 7
Discovered tracking at 10.

As a teenager, I saw images on T.V.
Black people dodging billy clubs,
Being swept down streets by fire hoses
Giving up limbs to police dogs
And dying—being hung, mutilated, destroyed
I've learned that women
are beaten, raped, murdered,
stepped over, stepped on, stomped
impoverished & dehumanized
I watched men like
Martin, Medgar, & Malcolm fall
and see Nazis and skinheads rise

I watched a government shrug it's shoulders
while AIDS run wild in the streets

and dope disseminates the minds
and bodies of children.

The white man has tried to convince me
that slaves were happy,
that negroes preferred segregation
and woman love to be dominated by men.
Now he wants me to ignore
the smog in my air—
the pesticides on my food—
the asbestos radon in my house
the madness in my society—
and believe—
I have cancer cause
I want it—
yeah.

# Trying to do how mama did can un Do you

**Prologue**

I don't know about you,
I know about me—
I remember— as a child
watching my mama—
and I came to certain
Conclusions.
Her life was not going
to be mine—
Call it childish clarity
or aimful ambition
one thing for certain
I wasn't going to be like my mama,
What I didn't know
couldn't seem to see—there was
no way that could ever be
Now I have to admit
with a lot more respect
Trying to do how mama did it
can undo you.

**I.**

Trying to do
How mama did
Can undo you

                    Remember when she said
                    some day you'll
                    mark my words

I remember
Mama used to
work washing floors

Then she came home
and cooked dinner
and cleaned house
and was mama

        That's simple stuff
        until you do it

I, first realized
Mama's power
I tried
to cook a
pot of gumbo

        Gumbo—
        a southern
        dish consisting
        of seafood,
        sausage, okra, and
        chicken, served
        over rice—
        a working class
        bouillabaise

Mama's gumbo
drove me nuts
I couldn't get
it dirty—
Could NOT find
that dishwater look

Mama didn't believe
in writing recipes
called her up once
and asked—
how do I cook this?

        Well daughter,
        you take a
        pinch of this
        and a little
        less than a

handful of that
and a smidgen
of . . .
I tried though
Got 2nd degree burns
from hot water cornbread—
ruined a whole sack of
potatoes trying to get
sweet potato salad—
and biscuits and gravy . . .
Trying to do
how mama
did can
un Do
you

II.

Mama used
to be off on Tuesday
I'd come from
school and the
house would be
gleaming—
Food on the stove— And
all the drawers
filled with
fresh washed,
clothes—
Closets filled
with ironed
and starched
blouses and
dresses,
immaculate—
At first she washed
by hand — a

                    scrub board and
                    a tin tub
                    later — She got
                    a washer—
                    finger type—
                    never did use
                    a dryer
                    except the sun.

I tried, mama
I got up early on my
day off— Gathered
the clothes—
Loaded the washer
Then swept all
the floors — broke
out the mop & 409 —
the oven cleaner —
the sponges —

                    Mama used
                    to make her
                    own soap

Put the second
load in the washer
Folded the first
Started scrubbing
the kitchen cabinets —

                    Mama used to
                    scrub all the
                    walls— wash
                    the venetian blinds
                    and can fruits &
                    vegetables on
                    her day off
I got the kitchen cleaned—
smiled at the like
Sun on a waxed fender
but it was 1 o'clock
and I was exhausted—

Trying to do
like mama did
can undo you

III.

After work,
She'd come home
cook dinner and
wait on Daddy
hand and foot

        A man's home
        is his castle, child
        keep it well and
        he won't stray

When I first got married
I'd run home from work
Cook dinner —
but after a while
that got too tacky

He wanted ironed
shirts, starched.
Dinner ready at
7. And wanted
me to go to bed
with him too.

        Mama used
        to iron the sheets
        and Daddy's shorts
        too.

I finally decided
that either mama
was an amazon
or nuts or
Daddy was crazy
but my old man had to go.

Trying to do
like mama
did can
undo you

**IV.**

I like kids,
I love my daughter
but sometimes —
She drives me nuts

Mama had 8
kids — 3
died in childhood

At least once,
every other week
the kid runs out
of socks or panties—
or they get lost—
I don't know how
but she loses them

Every Tuesday
all our clothes
were put in
our drawers
for the week
socks matched—
on the right
underwear
on the left.
ironed blouses
folded in
the middle.

I try to cook
balance meals
but sometimes
I have to break

out the hot dogs
and chili — or
get pizza or
Kentucky fried—
I'm just too
whipped to cook.

> Mama raised
> five — I had
> my first take out
> food when I was 17
> on a trip to California

**V.**

> "It's nice to be
> nice"

I hated that expression
when my sisters took my things
and I took revenge

> "It's nice to be
> nice"

When my friends broke my toys
and I tried to break their faces

> "It's nice to be
> nice"

When my father punished
me for nothing— and I
sulked for 3 days.

> "It's nice to be
> nice"

I decided one week
to do like mama
did—
no matter what was said,
no matter what deed done,
I would respond with kindness

I got a parking ticket—
The bank lost my paycheck—
My fender got crushed
in the parking lot,
when I started parking
to avoid getting any more
parking tickets.
I got cut in front of,
in the supermarket line.
I started getting an
ulcer—
Decided to respond
in kind—

> Trying to do
> like mama did—
> can un do you

What's certain for sure
is I am not my mama—
Things she did—
I cannot do—
but I do a few things
Mama couldn't do
She never saw a subway
or knew how to fend off a pass
or balance a check book
or tell a racist to
kiss her ass

Yeah — mama and I
are different folk

move through life
in stranger ways
but I've always
loved her
and now I
know — respect
is due her
for the way she did—
I'm a witness
these facts are true
Trying to do—
like mama did
can undo you.

# Note from the Editor

*The Complete Works of Pat Parker* gathers all of Pat Parker's published work from two books (*Movement in Black* and *Jonestown & Other Madness*) and three chapbooks (*Child of Myself*, *Pit Stop*, and *Womanslaughter*) with other previously unpublished poems, two plays, and a handful of prose essays. *The Complete Works of Pat Parker* is the most comprehensive presentation of Parker's work. In this Note, I outline how and why I made various decisions in assembling this text and point to some future directions for Parker scholarship.

Pat Parker's *Movement in Black* was her protean work, her most frequently published and widely distributed book. Parker first assembled *Movement in Black* in 1978. Diana Press published it in a cloth edition along side Judy Grahn's *The Work of a Common Woman*. The publishers of Diana Press, Coletta Reid and Casey Czarnik, wanted to ensure that the west coast feminist voices of Parker and Grahn were as visible as east coast poets Audre Lorde and Adrienne Rich. Lorde wrote the introduction to Parker's *Movement in Black*. Rich wrote the introduction to Grahn's *The Work of a Common Woman*. Shortly after publication, Diana Press encountered difficulties; by early 1979, the press ceased operations. This development curtailed the circulation of both Parker's and Grahn's books. In 1983, Crossing Press published a second edition of *Movement in Black* as a paperback using the original plates. After Parker's death in 1989, Nancy Bereano of Firebrand Books published a third edition from the original plates of the Diana Press and Crossing Press editions; the release of this third edition in 1990 corresponded with what would have been Parker's forty-sixth birthday, January 20, 1990. In 1999, Bereano published a commemorative edition of *Movement in Black* on the tenth anniversary of Parker's death; it featured tributes to Parker by Donna Allegra, Angela Y. Davis, Toi Derricotte, Jewelle Gomez, Audre

Lorde, Michelle Parkerson, Ann Allen Shockley, Barbara Smith, Pamela Sneed, and Evelyn C. White. Cheryl Clarke wrote the "Introduction."

The title poem, "Movement in Black," is a poem and a spoken word / performance piece. Alberta Jackson, Pat Parker, Vicki Randle, Linda Tillery, and Mary Watkins first performed "Movement in Black" at the Oakland Auditorium on December 2-3, 1977. Parker performed "Movement in Black" with other women during the following year on the "Varied Voices of Black Women" tour organized by Olivia Records. As a poet, Parker performed on the page and the stage—as well as on vinyl. The album, *Where Would I Be Without You*, featured Parker and Grahn reading from their work.

For *The Complete Works of Pat Parker*, *Movement in Black* remains a centerpiece of Parker's work. The poems of *Movement in Black* open this book. The 1978/1983/1990 editions of *Movement in Black* are all identical except for front matter; these editions are the basis of the presentation of poems from *Movement in Black* for this edition. The "New Poems" from the 1999 edition are reproduced as they appear in that edition. Following *Movement in Black* is the complete reproduction of *Jonestown & Other Madness*. *Jonestown* has been less in the public eye as representative of Parker's work, but this collection of poetry is extraordinary; Parker blends the documentary, narrative, and lyrical impulses of poetry in powerful ways in this work.

Following these two collections are four sections of additional work by Parker. Parker wrote a number of prose pieces, both fiction and creative non-fiction; many are collected here. She wrote two plays; both, "Hard Time" and "Pinocle" are presented here. "Restored Poems" appeared in Parker's earlier chapbooks, but she omitted them from *Movement in Black* when she assembled it in 1978. An appendix contains the tables of contents for *Child of Myself*, *Pit Stop*, and *Womanslaughter* with notes about these editions. Using these tables and the "Restored Poems," readers can revisit Parker's earlier ordering of the poems.

"Uncollected Poems" have not appeared in Parker's previously published books. Many of these poems were published or performed during Parker's lifetime. These poems appear in roughly chronological order according to when she composed them. They are divided into three sections, 1960s, 1970s, and 1980s. Where possible, I have indicated the approximate year of composition; a "m" indicates the poem existed in manuscript form only; a "p" indicates that Parker published the poem." Some critics may question to decision to publish some of the previously unpublished materials. Through feminist and lesbian publications, Parker had many opportunities to publish her work; what remained unpublished may have been incomplete in her eyes. That may be true, but during the final two years of her life, illness hampered Parker's creative production and her ability to publish and promote her work. The breadth of creative output collected here demonstrates the seriousness of Parker's overall work as a writer. Beginning in 1963, when she was nineteen years old, and continuing until she died in 1989, Parker took her work as a writer seriously. Gathering as much of it as possible into a single volume invites readers to take it seriously as well.

There are a few notable omissions from this collection. In Parker's papers, there are numerous typewritten manuscript pages for a novel that she was writing at the time of her death. This manuscript is worth further examination. During her final months, Parker went to Washington, DC, to speak at a lesbian conference. A fair copy of this speech "Aging and Ageism in a Multicultural Multiracial Lesbian Society," is available in her archives; it merits further attention.

As these omissions indicate, despite the title, this collection is not, in fact, complete. Throughout the end notes are flags of missing materials and suggestions about where additional textual and scholarly work on Parker remains. I hope that other readers, writers, and critics will engage with Parker and her archives at The Arthur and Elizabeth Schlesinger Library on the History of Women in America to discover and share a more complete understanding of her legacy. While complete may be a misnomer, this edition is the most complete assembly of Pat Parker's work to date; it invites readers to dig deeper into her rich creative output.

The end notes that follow have two objectives. First, they provide helpful guidance to readers encountering Parker for the first time. Explanations of allusions and references in the text are in the end notes as well as suggestions for additional reading. Second, the end notes provide space for me to be transparent about how I edited this book. I invite readers to interrogate rigorously my decisions in the creation of the text. Editing an author's work posthu-mously is a fraught project. Editorial power is not to be used lightly, particularly for a white woman, like me, editing an African-Ameri-can woman, like Parker. Through the end notes, I highlight where I made editorial choices and, particularly where I made line edits, changing what was in the original, published text or in manuscript.

Close engagements with Parker's work convince me even more of her significance as a poet and writer and of her compelling vision as an artist. Parker worked hard throughout her life to fulfill her artistic calling. She left behind an impressive corpus for readers and writers to engage. I hope that this book honors her and her work.

Julie R. Enszer, PhD
May 2016

Pat Parker and Cheryl Clarke after a joint reading at Cal State/ LA in March 1989

# End Notes

Two images appeared in *Movement in Black*: Aya and Nkyimkyim. Aya is "the fern, a symbol of defiance." It is the separate mark between sections in the table of contents of this book. Nkyim-kyim is "twisted pattern, meaning changing one's self or playing many parts." It appears as the separator mark between sections of *Movement in Black*.

*Movement in Black*

General Notes

The text from *Movement in Black* is from the 1978/83/90 editions, which all appear to have used the same plates, though each was published by a different publisher.

The 1999 edition of *Movement in Black* includes substantial changes to the poems, including the addition of many titles to poems previously untitled.

While this text shows fealty to the text in the 1978/83/90 editions, I insert em dashes where earlier texts used hyphens. Typography and typesetting have evolved substantially since the first assembly of *Movement in Black* in 1978. Readers' engagements with screens, word processing programs, and other digital tools create new expectations for typesetting and design. Where the hyphens used in the 1978/83/90 editions suggest space and a breath for readers in those eras, readers today are more sensitive to em dashes, en dashes, hyphens and their divergent gestures. The em dash seems overall more inline with the type of pause that Parker imagined for readers.

Hyphenated words offer various editorial choices. Generally, I have preserved Parker's hyphenation or lack of hyphenation in the poems. As I have edited this volume, I have wondered how hyphenation of words and word phrases relates to the performative aspects of many of these poems.

Parker's capitalization is capricious throughout *Movement in Black*. She uses I and i variably and to my reading inconsistently; similarly 'and' and '&.' There are numerous other examples of Parker's engagement with capitalization. In some instances, capitalization or lack of capitalization seems a clear statement on power and authority within the text, for instance capitalizing "Black." In other instances, the meanings are less clear. The text here reflects how the poems were presented in the 1978/83/90 editions; the 1999 edition standardizes some of these choices. Thinking about the differences in presentation between the texts is a productive activity.

In reproducing Parker's poems for this edition, I have tried to hew closely to previously published works and to manuscript and typewritten copy of the poems. As with dashes and hyphens, however, the production of print material has changed substantially since Parker's work. As an early member of the Women's Press Collective, Parker was attuned keenly to the physical aspects of book-making, including typography and typesetting. Many of her indentations in the poems are small—a few spaces. I wonder if she might have rethought the physical presentation of her poetry on the page as personal computers and desktop publishing evolved. She did not live to see this rapid evolution. The physical presentation on the page is as faithful as possible to its production from the 1970s, but I often wonder if she would want more bold spaces in her work given the availability of technology today.

### Notes on the Poems

This edition of Parker's master work includes Audre Lorde's introduction to the 1978 and 1984 editions of *Movement in Black*. While Parker's respect for Lorde was great and their friendship significant to both women, Parker did not like the phrase in Lorde's introduction that suggested that her poems had lines that faltered. Nevertheless, this introduction to Parker's work is significant because of Lorde's reputation and many commendations of Parker's work and their enduring, nearly twenty year friendship.

The 1999 edition of *Movement in Black* includes an "Introduction" by Cheryl Clarke and celebrations, remembrances, and tributes by Donna Allegra, Angela Y. Davis, Toi Derricotte, Jewelle Gomez,

Audre Lorde, Michelle Parkerson, Ann Allen Shockley, Barbara Smith, Pamela Sneed, and Evelyn C. White. These pieces are not reproduced in this edition; all are wonderful and worth reading.

In "Goat Child," there are not dates in the second part of the poem in the 1978/83/90 editions; they are inserted {1956-1962} in the 1999 edition, providing consistency among the sections. For this edition, I did not insert them.

In [from cavities of bone], the 1978/83/90 editions have the Genesis quotation as 1:23; it is actually 2:23. It is corrected in this edition.

"Brother" was used in the television show *A Different World* on April 2, 1992. Nancy Bereano of Firebrand Books negotiated a cash payment for the use of the poem and a t-shirt, cast photo, and copy of the script for Anastasia, Parker's daughter with Marty Dunham. Anastasia was ten years old when the episode aired.

In "Dialogue," Parker inserts an asterisk at the line "Child, dear child, I must," and attributes it to Shirley Jones, her sister. I have removed the asterisk attribution from this edition after reader reports that it was distracting. An early manuscript copy of this poem presents the third line in the sixth stanza as "First, you stop smoking pot."

In "Pied Piper," the third line from the end in the 1978/83/90 edition reads: "Yes, does it mean?" The 1999 edition inserts the word "what" which clarifies meaning for readers. I have used this correction in this edition.

The "Mau Mau" reference at the end of this poem refers to the uprising in Kenya by Kikuyu leaders against British rule.

In the poem [I'm so tired], in the penultimate line, in the 1978/83/90 edition, the singular verb is used. In the 1999 edition, the lines are "the tactics / of this revolution / are to / talk the enemy to death." The grammatical change is correct, yet there is a plea-sure to the vernacular in the earlier formation, so I let it remain for this edition.

In [Boots are being polished], M.C.C. refers to the Metropolitan Community Church, an evangelical Christian church that ministers to LGBT people. MCC began in Los Angeles and has grown since its founding to now be the largest LGBT Christian denomination in the United States.

"The *What* Liberation Front?" playfully suggests Parker's affection for her canine companions. See the photograph of Parker and one of her dogs on page 299.

In the poem [I have a dream], Martin refers to Martin Luther King, Jr., Malcolm refers to Malcolm X, Huey refers to Huey P. Newton, co-founder of the Black Panther Party, George refers to George Jackson, a prison activist killed by guards at the San Quentin Prison, and Angela refers to Angela Y. Davis, an African-American activist, prisoner, author, lesbian, and feminist.

In "Movement in Black," in the third stanza of the second part, all editions read "shot a few man too." I believe Parker meant men and have corrected that in this edition.

This note is included about "Movement in Black": This poem was first performed at Oakland Auditorium on December 2$^{nd}$ and 3$^{rd}$ 1977 by Linda Tillery, Vicki Randle, Alberta Jackson, Mary Watkins and Pat Parker.

The original artwork by Irmagean in the 1978/83/90 edition is powerful and adds to the poem. It is worth seeking out an earlier edition to see the art-word combination as part of Parker's vision of this poem.

Marie Cooks in the poem "Cop-out" is Parker's mother.

Willyce in the poem "For Willyce" is the Asian-American poet Willyce Kim, author of three books of poetry, *Curtains of Light* (1970), *Eating Artichokes* (1972), and *Under the Rolling Sky* (1976).

In the poem [Let me come to you naked], the refrain line in the quatrains originally appears as "and lay beside you." This is corrected, grammatically, in the 1999 edition, yet I delight in the assonance of lay and I suspect Parker might have. Both the assonance and the punning of lay bring joy in spite of its grammar. I think readers will enjoy the pleasure and overlook the error (if it is an error).

Gente is a Spanish word that means people. Parker's poem "gente" refers to gathering with other women of color. Gente was also a San Francisco Bay Area organization of women of color that Parker belonged to and was active with during her life.

"Womanslaughter" is about the murder of Parker's sister Shirley Jones.

New Work

Nancy Bereano assembled the poems in the section of *Movement in Black* titled "New Work" for the 1999 edition. In doing the research for this edition of Parker's work, I did not review the material that Bereano worked with to assemble the 1999 edition. This section is a fair transcription of the published poems. I hope that another scholar will review those materials and think and write bout the editorial interventions in these poems, further engaging Parker's work and the editorial relationships among lesbian-feminist authors and publishers.

Parker's poem "Progeny" references multiple activists of the civil rights movement, beginning with Medgar Evers, Martin Luther King, Jr, and Malcolm X, and their daughters (Parker later references Ms. Shabazz, Malcolm X's daughter, directly). In the fifth stanza, Parker lists four African-Americans who were killed by police. The New York City police shot and killed Eleanor Bumpurs in her Bronx apartment in 1984; Clifford Glover was shot and killed by a New York police officer in 1973; a Detroit policewoman killed Allene Richardson outside of her apartment building; a New York City police officer killed Randy Evans in 1976. Parker reference the mothers of Emmett Till, Bobby Hutton, and Jonathan Jackson, two of who were killed in armed struggles on behalf of Black freedom struggles. With these multiple references, Parker constructs a genealogy of thirty years from the death of Till in 1955 through the death of Eleanor Bumpurs.

The epigraph to "For Audre" is from Audre Lorde's poem, "The Black Unicorn," which appeared in her 1978 collection of the same title. The later epigraph from "A Woman Speaks" is also from Lorde's *The Black Unicorn* (New York: W.W. Norton, 1978). Spinsters Ink published *The Cancer Journals* by Audre Lorde in 1980. Persephone Press published *Zami: A New Spelling of My Name* in 1982.

"Funny" is a brief memoir piece that appeared at the end of the posthumous edition of *Movement in Black*. One of the hallmarks of literary activism among lesbian-feminists is the blurring of genres. Poetry, prose, memoir, novels, fiction, and non-fiction all blended in vital and productive ways in the worlds of writers like Parker. Throughout the 1980s, Parker wrote prose pieces—short stories, a novel, and other pieces of prose, including numerous speeches. "Funny" is preserved with *Movement in Black* in this edition of Parker's work. Additional prose is included in a separate section. Parker worked on "Funny" in her journal with the title "The Closet Chronicles" and the piece opens with the date 1955.

The final line of "Funny," 'we would not have to walk alone,' seems to echo Marijane Meeker (Ann Aldrich's) iconic nonfiction book about lesbianism in the 1950s, *We Walk Alone* (1955).

*Jonestown & other madness*

In the 1970s, Parker was involved in the production of her work as a member of the Women's Press Collective and, later, with Diana Press. When Firebrand Books published *Jonestown & other madness*, Parker wanted an African American woman to design the cover. Nancy Bereano wrote to Pat Parker on November 5, 1984, "I have located a Black woman designer to do the cover for JONESTOWN AND OTHER MADNESS. It turns out that she (Cassandra Maxwell-Simmons) has a sister in San Francisco who was going to be sent to Jonestown to cover the massacre by the television station she works for, but her passport was out of date. In any case, she is reading the manuscript and coming up with ideas." (Division of Rare and Manuscript Collections, Cornell University Library, Firebrand Books records, 1984-2000 Box 8, Folder "Jonestown & other madness General 84-85," Letter to Pat Parker from Nancy Bereano).

Jonestown foreword: Jonestown was the name of a settlement in Guyana led by Jim Jones. On November 18, 1978, over 900 people committed suicide in a tragedy that was widely reported throughout the United States.

Blackberri is a singer, composer, poet, photographer, and political activist based in Oakland, CA.

On Thanksgiving Day in 1980, Priscilla Ford used her car to kill six people and injure twenty-three others in downtown Las Vegas. The newspaper article image on page 207 is from the papers of Pat Parker at the Schlesinger library.

*Prose*

"The Demonstrator" appeared in a series in *Negro Digest* titled, "All for the Cause" in the November 1963 issue. Parker published under the name P. A. Bullins. Bullins was her married name at the time. She published three other essays under the name P. A. Bullins in *Black Dialogue*, *Perspectives* and *Citadel* (the literary magazine of Los Angeles Community College).

In "The Demonstrator," CORE refers to the Congress of Racial Equality. Founded in 1942, CORE played a pivotal role in the civil rights struggles of the 1950s and 1960s.

"Autobiography Chapter One" appeared in *True to Life Adventure Stories, volume two*. Parker was working on an autobiography project during the 1980s, though she never completed the project.

"Shoes" appeared in *True to Life Adventure Stories*, edited by Judy Grahn (Oakland, CA: Diana Press, 1978): 176-182. It was reprinted in *I Never Told Anyone* with the following epigraph:

Pat Parker, from "I Never Told Anyone"

"At nine years old, being a black child in the South in the 1950s, it was impossible for my story to have any other ending, and that still makes me angry."

*Pat Parker was born on January 20, 1944, in Houston, Texas, where her story "Shoes", takes place. About the story, she writes: "I felt the need to get it out of my system in order to move on to other things. I had never told the story to anyone. I carried a great deal of anger as a result of the incident: anger toward my parents for their insistence that I respect any adult as an authority figure; anger toward the store owner for this perversion and use of me; and anger at the economic structure of this political system."*

*She continues: "I still have thoughts from time to time of returning to Houston and seeing if that store is still there. I often wonder about the store owner and his family. And I wonder how many other little girls, long after I left the school, were invited to see the shoes.*

*"Shoes" was originally published in* True to Life Adventure Stories, *edited by Judy Grahn and published by Diana Press. Four books of poetry by Pat Parker have also been published, and she has appeared on three record albums and in numerous anthologies. Currently she is at work on her fifth book of poetry as well as a novel and a play. She is also a director of the Oakland Feminist Health Center in Oakland, California.*

In the text of "Shoes," Parker refers to Buster Brown and Ty in the *True to Life Adventure Stories* edition; in *I Never Told Anyone*, the editors reformat this section and refer to the dog as Tyge. I believe that the spelling of Buster Brown's dog's name is Tige. I have let Parker's spelling stand and used the original version from *True to Life Adventure Stories*.

Judy Grahn accepted the short story, "Mama and the Hogs," for a third volume of *True to Life Adventure Stories*. This volume was never published. Judy Grahn generously provided me with her co-pyedited copy of the story for inclusion in this edition.

"Revolution: It's Not Neat or Pretty or Quick" appeared in *This Bridge Called My Back*, edited by Cherríe Moraga and Gloria Anzaldúa (Watertown, MA: Persephone Press, 1981 and New York: Kitchen Table: Women of Color Press, 1983): 238-42. Parker refers on page 254 to the Iranian Revolution in 1979 that replaced the Shah with Khomeini, the leader of the revolution. Parker also mentions Iran in the play "Pinocle" on page 304 and in the poem "[Every once in a while]" on page 403. Parker references the fifty-two American diplomats and citizens who were held hostage in Iran from November 1979 through January 1981. The Trilateral Commission was founded in 1973 "to foster closer cooperation among North America, Western Europe, and Japan. At the end of "Revolution," Parker references Judy Grahn's "She Who" poems. Diana Press first published *She Who*: *A Graphic Book of Poems* in 1977; many of the poems from the collection are included in Grahn's new and selected poems, *love belongs to those who do the feeling* (Red Hen Press, 2008).

"Poetry at Women's Music Festivals: Oil and Water," *Hot Wire* (November 1986): 52-53; 63. Toni Armstrong, Michele Gautreaux, Ann Morris, and Yvonne Zipter founded *Hot Wire: A Journal of Women's Music and Culture* and published the first issue in November 1984. Toni Armstrong acted as the publisher and managing editor through its ten year publication, ending in September 1994. Parker's article, "Poetry at Women's Music Festivals: Oil and Water" was a part of the RE:INKING series. Hot Wire described the series this way, "Re:Inking articles deal with women's writing as a cultural phenomenon, including individual writers, women's publishing ventures and the growing Women-In-Print movement."

The National Women's Music Festival, a four-day musical and cultural gathering, began in 1975. Parker performed at the Festival and was scheduled to perform at the Festival in June 1989, but she was too sick to travel to Bloomington, Indiana, where it was held that year. On page 262, the original article contains this line: "bar women would not give up their junkboxes." Perhaps Parker meant juke boxes or perhaps it was a neologism by Parker commenting on the music.

Olivia Records was a woman-owned music company that produced records and concerts from 1973 until 1988; in 1988 it became a lesbian travel company. Parker and Grahn's album,

Where Would I Be Without You, was the only spoken word album produced by Olivia Records. For more information about the album see Clarke and Enszer, "Introduction." For more information about Olivia Records, see Bonnie Morris, "Olivia Records: The Production of a Movement," *Journal of Lesbian Studies* 19, no. 3 (Summer 2015): 290-304.

For more information about the Varied Voices of Black Women tour, see Michelle Moravec's manuscript in progress here: http://politicsofwomensculture.michellemoravec.com/varied-voices-of-black-women-an-evening-of-words-and-music-writinginpublic-spring-2016/.

"Gay Parenting, Or, Look out, Anita," appeared in *Politics of the Heart: A Lesbian Parenting Anthology*, edited by Sandra Pollack and Jeanne Vaughn (Ithaca, NY: Firebrand, 1987), 94-99.

Anita in the title is a reference to Anita Bryant, the spokeswoman for Florida oranges who lead an anti-gay and lesbian campaign in the late 1970s.

"The 1987 March on Washington: The Morning Rally" describes Parker's experiences at the second national march for gay and lesbian rights on October 11, 1987 in Washington, DC. *Hot Wire* published this piece in January 1989. In the text box on page 272, Kathy Tsui is, I believe, an error in the original article. Kitty Tsui was a speaker at the morning rally along with Parker. Morris Kight was a gay rights pioneer and peace activist based in Los Angeles, California. Buffy Dunker was a Boston-based lesbian activist who was profiled in Ginny Vida's *Our Right to Love: A Lesbian Resource Book*. ARC is an acronym for AIDS-related complex, a term commonly used in the late 1980s to describe AIDS-related illnesses.

*Two Plays*

"Hard Time"

It is unclear from Parker's archive when she wrote this play. She did have a clean copy in her papers with some small edits. It may have been written as early as 1965 or 1966 or as late as the mid-1970s.

A list of characters inserted for clarity.

The name of the protagonist of "Hard Time" is Uhuru, a Swahili word for freedom. Most likely for Parker it also nodded to international socialism centered in Africa.

"Pinochle"

It is unclear from Parker's archive when she drafted this play. The version presented here is clearly labeled first draft and the text itself seems less unified than "Hard Times." One can imagine Parker editing and polishing this play further. Yet, in conversation with "Hard Times," "Pinochle" demonstrates her interest in the genre of playwriting and the development of her concerns as a writer.

A list of characters inserted for clarity.

*Restored Poems*

When Parker assembled Movement in Black, she deleted two poems from *Child of Myself*, "Assassination" and "Ice Cream Blues," and one poem from *Pit Stop*: "To an Unlabelled." These three poems are presented in the "Restored Poems" section of the book. For original tables of contents of all of Parker's chapbooks including textual notes on the chapbooks and their different printings, see Appendix.

Uncollected Poems: 1960s, 1970s, 1980s

These poems are arranged in approximate chronological order based on dates indicated on manuscript or typewritten pages, the order of the poems in Parker's papers, and information gleaned from letters and journals. Where possible, I indicate dates from Parker's papers. A "m" indicates that the poem was transcribed from a manuscript copy; a "p" indicates that Parker published the poem.

These poems are presented by and large without editorial interventions. When I have inserted a word or altered the text, I indicate the change with [brackets].

As with *Movement in Black*, where Parker used a hyphen on the typewriter, I have inserted an em dash.

Two notebooks in Parker's papers—a red notebook and a black notebook—contain drafts of Parker's poems. In both of these note-books, Parker has drafts of poems that she published during her lifetime. In the red notebook, there are drafts of "Child's Play," "Georgia, Georgia / Georgia on My Mind," "love isn't," "Trying to do How Mama Did can Un Do you," "Bar Conversation," "My Brother," "Legacy," "Aftermath," "For Audre," "For Wayne," "Massage," and "Reputation." Drafts of "Timothy Lee" and "Oprah Winfrey" are in the red notebook; a draft of "[little Billy Tipton]" is in the black notebook. Examining early drafts of these poems might illuminate more about Parker's creative process and textual attention to the manuscript drafts might inform modes of thinking about editorial processes in feminist presses.

Uncollected Poems: 1960s

In the poem "The Mirror," a typographic error in the first line appears in the published text "gleaminng"; it is corrected for this edition.

"The Mirror" and "Of Life" appeared in *The Citadel*, the literary magazine of the Los Angeles Community College, in the fall of 1964. Pat Bullins was the poetry editor.

"[I have seen death]" appeared in *Black Dialogue*, vol. 1, no. 3&4 (Winter 1966), under her married name Pat Bullins. The then Patricia Cooks married playwright Ed Bullins in 1962.

"To a Friend," "City Song," "Not a Good Night," and "Poem to my Mother" appeared in the journal *Perspectives* in 1965 with this biographical statement: Patricia Bullins is 21 years old. Lives in San Francisco. Is a writing major at San Francisco State College, but will change to History because she doesn't like being told how to write. Primary goal is to be accepted as a "good poet", not just a "good woman poet". Has appeared in "Negro Digest", "Citadel", and "Black Dialogue". Soon to appear in "Dust".

"To a Poet, dead," "Please you all," "Two Faces of Black," "Gold Stars & Hollow Bags," and [A sea haw soars above my head.]" appeared in *Perspectives* in 1965 under the name Patricia Bullins with this biographical statement: Patricia Bullins has two cats, Squibob and Loven. At night, Squibob sleeps on her head. Loren sleeps on Squibob's head. These are truly talented cats, for Patricia sleeps hanging by her feet from the chandelier.

[Two people walk], "Snatches of a Day," and "Berkeley '66" appeared in the literary journal *Out of Sight* in August 1966 under the name Patricia Parker.

"Confrontation" is a fair transcription of the poem from the typewritten manuscript. For example, there is a space before the explanation point in the first line; in the third line from the end can and not are two separate words. I present this poem—and others in this section—without editorial interventions for readers to experience a closer relationship to Parker's artistic production. "Confrontation" first appeared in the literary journal *Litmus*.

"With Love to Lyndon" is signed Patricia Bullins. Ed Bullins was Parker's first husband and she took his name when they married.

"Summer" contains a marking on the page indicating that Parker worked on this poem in 1965.

"From the Wars" is dated June 20, 1965 in the manuscript copy used for this transcription.

"To a Deaf Poet" is dated July 7, 1965 and signed Patricia Bullins.

[Two people walk] is dated December 29, 1965 and signed Patricia Bullins.

[Why burn a candle in daylight?] is dated August 19, 1966 and signed Patricia Parker.

"Anatomy of a Pig" is dated March 30, 1976.

Parker made two handwritten corrections in "Going to the bridge now." In the second stanza the typewritten word woman is changed to dykes by hand. In the final stanza, the typewritten manuscript readers, "Said I would kill myself," in the first and third line. Handwritten over it is the contraction I'd. The printed text includes these handwritten corrections.

[There are so many bags to fall in] is dated October 1969.

Uncollected Poems: 1970s

"Speech by a Black Nationalist to a white Audience." is dated August 1970.

[ i will not always be with you] is dated August 1970 and marked revised August 26, 1970.

[not by chance] is dated July 28, 1969 and marked revised August 25, 1970.

"A Woman's Love" is signed Patricia Parker.

[i have seen], "To Lynda," and [from my bedroom window] are transcribed from manuscript pages held in the Lynda Koolish Photographs Collection at the San Francisco Public Library.

"Sunday Morning" is marked revised August 27, 1974.

"To Tamara (Tami) Kallen)" is dated October 5, 1974.

"Gente" is dated November 30, 1974.

"Cop took my hand" is dated May 7, 1975.

The limericks were all written on a small notepad advertising Cleocin Phosphate.

"Poem for Ann #5" is dated June 28, 1975.

[i must learn] is from a manuscript page with the number two at the top suggesting that it is the end of a longer poem.

"well, I got the menstrual blues," "my baby's a bass player," and "[I fell in love some time ago]" are song lyrics. At one point Parker wanted to write song lyrics more than poems because of the economic potential of songs over poems. Tassaway is a cup for capturing menstrual fluids; the manufacturer of Tassaway advertised it in the early 1970s.

Two early drafts of [I fell in love some time ago] are in Parker's red notebook. One draft is a couplet:

> Is your closet door a squeaking
> when you're cripping out at night

In this couplet, Parker crossed out slipping and replaced it with cripping.

The second draft is a set of couplets; it appears on a separate page in the journal:
> I can't help but wonder
> when you kiss & hold me tight
> Is your closet door a squeaking
> when you're slipping out at night

In "A Walk," the typewritten manuscript misspells adolescence; it is corrected in this presentation.

In "At first, I," in the fourteenth line, it is difficult to read the handwriting—I used the word specter. Richard Milhous referenced in this poem is Richard Milhous Nixon.

Uncollected Poems: 1980s

"For Wayne" contains this note in the upper right hand corner of the typewritten manuscript: "Faggot: A bundle of sticks, twigs or small branches of trees used for fuel".

Oprah Winfrey began her show in Chicago in January 1984 and the show syndicated nationally in September 1986.

"Reflections on a March" is dated 10/21/87 in Parker's notebook. The Second National March on Washington for Lesbian and Gay Rights happened on October 11, 1987. Parker performed on the stage.

"To My Straight Sister" was handwritten in Parker's red journal and a typewritten copy exists in Parker's archive. The reproduced copy of this copy is from the typewritten copy.

Timothy Lee was hung to death on November 2, 1985 in Concord, CA, a predominantly white suburb east of San Francisco. Timothy Lee was a 23-year old Black Gay man. Lee's death occurred the same night as a stabbing attack on two Black men by two whites wearing Ku Klux Klan-type robes. At the behest of the local chapter of the NAACP, the FBI investigated both cases. This description comes from an Update by Elizabeth Pincus in *Black/ Out: The Magazine of the National Black Lesbian and Gay Leadership Coalition*, vol 1, no 3/4 (1987). The Update is reprinted from *Gay Community News*.

[little Billy Tipton] must have been one of the final poems that Parker composed. Tipton died on January 21, 1989, less than six months before Parker did. News of him passing as a man quickly spread, likely prompting Parker to compose this poem. For more information about Billy Tipton's life, see Diane Wood Middlebrook's biography of Tipton, *Suits Me: The Double Life of Billy Tipton* (Boston: Houghton Mifflin Company, 1998).

Three poems came from the black notebook in Parker's papers: [We're the Dunham-Parker's from Pleasant Hill], [It's not so bad], [There are those].

[We're the Dunham-Parker's from Pleasant Hill] is an occasional poem that Parker composed and performed for her inlaw's fiftieth wedding anniversary.

[It's not so bad] was written in the black notebook. A typewritten copy is in the archive as well. The version reproduced here is from the typewritten copy. This poem was dated January 20, 1989, which was the last birthday Parker was alive.

Multiple iterations of the long poem "Trying to do how mama did can un Do you" are in Parker's papers. This poem is presented as the last poem of this section as it was frequently performed and Parker seemed to be working on it intensively in the last years of her life. Parker performed this poem many times in the last five years of her life. Parker's partner, Marty Dunham remembers audiences reciting the chorus, "Trying to do / How mama did / Can undo you." This version of the poem is from a typewritten copy that seems to be the most complete based on my review of Parker's papers. The title is reproduced as she typed it.

In the fourth part, Parker typed whopped; I believe that she meant whipped and have changed it in this version; alternately she may have mean whooped.

Pat Parker and her partner, Marty Dunham

Pat Parker holding her daughter Cassidy Brown
with Marty Dunham holding their daughter Anastasia

# Acknowledgments

Thank you to Marty Dunham and Anastasia Dunham-Parker-Brady for saying yes to this edition of Pat Parker's work. They both have been careful stewards of Parker's papers and legacy over the past nearly thirty years; I am enormously appreciative for their labor and care on behalf of Parker and her papers. I also appreciate their general good cheer and companionship in my work on Parker's poetry, papers, and legacy. I hope that this edition of Parker's work fills you both with joy and love for her life and legacy which I know touches you every day. This book is dedicated to Parker's three grandchildren with the wish that they will know the powerful work of the grandmother they never met.

Cheryl Clarke and Judy Grahn have been important thought partners with me on all aspects of the preparation of this manuscript and the publication of this edition of Parker's work. I am grateful to both Cheryl and Judy for their support and assistance with this volume—and for their volumes of creative work and the model that they provide me and so many others as engaged, visionary poets.

Thank you to Lawrence Schimel for the partnership to publish the Sapphic Classics and for spearheading fundraising to support this volume. Thank you to all of the donors who contributed to publishing this book.

Thank you to the following students and interns who provided excellent transcriptions for the creation of this book: Maxx Bauman, Sarah Greaney, Rachel Lallouz, Caely McHale, and Asma Neblett.

Finally, thank you to my beloved Kim whose love and labor make my work possible.

All errors are, of course, my own.

# Bibliography

## POETRY COLLECTIONS

*Movement in Black* (Oakland, California: Diana Press, 1978; Trumansburg, New York: Crossing Press, 1983; Ithaca, New York: Firebrand Books, 1990, 1999).
*Jonestown & Other Madness* (Ithaca, New York: Firebrand Books 1985).
*Womanslaughter* (Oakland, California: Diana Press, 1978).
*Pit Stop* (Oakland, California: Women's Press Collective, 1974, 1975).
*Child of Myself* (San Lorenzo, California: Shameless Hussy Press, 1971; Oakland, California: Women's Press Collective, 1972, 1974).

## ANTHOLOGIES, MAGAZINE AND NEWSPAPER PUBLICATIONS

Parker's work appeared in multiple journals, magazines, newspapers and anthologies, including: *Loveletter* (1968); *Mark in Time, Portraits & Poetry / S. F.* (Glide Publications, 1971); *Mother Magazine* (December 1971); *Sun Dance Magazine* (November-December 1972); *Best Friends* 2 (University of New Mexico press, 1972); *The Furies* (June/July 1972); *Sisters Magazine* IV, no 9 (September 1973); *Woman to Woman*, edited by Judy Grahn and Wendy Cadden (Oakland, CA: Women's Press Collective, 1974); *Plexus* (April 1974); *San Francisco Feminist Journal* (May 1974); *Lesbian Tide* (July 1974); *Plexus* (January 1975); *Amazon Poetry*, edited by Elly Bulkin and Joan Larkin (Brooklyn, NY: Out & Out Press, 1975); *Crimes Against Women*, edited by Diana E. H. Russell and Nicole Van de Ven (Les Femmes, 1976); *Conditions: Five / The Black Women's Issue*, edited by Lorraine Bethel and Barbara

Smith (1979); *The Lesbian Path*, edited by Peg Cruikshank (Angel Press, 1980); *Lesbian Poetry*, edited by Elly Bulkin and Joan Larkin (Watertown, MA: Persephone Press, 1981).

## UNCOLLECTED EARLY POETRY

"The Mirror." *Citadel* (Fall 1964): 12 (published as Pat Bullins).
"Berkeley ' 66." *Out of Sight* (August 1966): 41.
"A Reply to J. Wilson." *Dust* no. 9 (Fall 1966): 39.
"Two People Walk into a Park." *Out of Sight* (August 1966): 39.
"A Walk." *Anthology of Poems Read at COSMEP, the Conference of Small Magazine Editors and Pressmen.* eds., Richard Kerch and John Oliver Simon. Berkeley: Noh Directions Press. 1968. 18-19.
"Assassination." *Dices or Black Bones: Black Voices of the 1970s.* Ed., Adam David Miller. Boston: Houghton Mifflin, 1970. 110.

## READINGS & PERFORMANCES
### 1989
California State University, Los Angeles, California (with Cheryl Clarke)

### 1984
Antioch College, Yellow Springs, Ohio
Pacific Center Benefit, Oakland, California
A Woman's Place Bookstore, Oakland, California (benefit for Pat Norman)
Evergreen State College, Olympia, Washington
San Francisco State University, San Francisco, California
New College, San Francisco, CA (benefit for Seminary)

### 1983
University of Oregon, Eugene, Oregon
La Pena Cultural Center, Oakland, California
LA Women's Building, Los Angeles, California
SF Women's Building, San Francisco, California

### 1982
Artemis, San Francisco, California
Black Historical Research Society, San Francisco, California

San Francisco Gay Pride Day, San Francisco, California
Unitarian Church, Denver, Colorado
University of Cincinnati, Cincinnati, Ohio

**1981**
Arlington Street Church, Boston, Massachusetts
Old Wives Tales, San Francisco, California
East Bay Gay Day, Oakland, California

**1980**
San Jose State University, San Jose, California
First Unitarian Church, Los Angeles, California
Lone Mountain State College, San Francisco, California
San Francisco State University, San Francisco, California

**1979**
Michigan State University, East Lansing, Michigan
California State University at Long Beach, Long Beach, California

**1978**
University of Rhode Island, Kingston, Rhode Island
Boston University, Boston, Massachusetts
Massachusetts Correctional Institution, Framington, Massachusetts
Vassar College, Poughkeepsie, New York
University of Massachusetts, Amherst, Massachusetts
University of Delaware, Newark, Delaware
St. George Methodist Church, Philadelphia, Pennsylvania
Rutgers University, New Brunswick, New Jersey
Ontario Theatre, Washington, DC
Medusa's Revenge, New York, New York

**1977**
Chico State University, Chico, California
University of Oregon, Eugene, Oregon
First Annual San Francisco Women's Poetry Festival, San Francisco,
    California
Washington State NOW Conference, Seattle, Washington

**1976**
International Tribunal on Crimes Against Women, Brussels, Belgium
Mills College, Oakland, California
University of Southern California, Los Angeles, California
Glide Memorial Church, San Francisco, California

**1975**
Fahrenheit 451 Bookstore, Laguna Beach, California
Las Hermanas, San Diego California
University of New Mexico, Albuquerque, New Mexico
Focus II Gallery, New York, New York
Yale University, New Haven, Connecticut
Club Madone, Washington, DC
First Unitarian Church, Cincinnati, Ohio
The Saints, Boston, Massachusetts
Houston Women's Center, Houston, Texas

**1974**
Evergreen State College, Olympia, Washington
University of California at Los Angeles, Los Angeles, California
NOW, Stockton, California
California Institute for Women, Ontario, California
Intersection, San Francisco, California
Mills College, Oakland, California
Santa Rosa Junior College, Santa Rosa, California

**1973**
Foothill College, Oakland, California
KQED-TV, San Francisco, California

**PROSE**

"The Demonstrator," *Negro Digest* (November 1963): 28-29.
"Autobiography: Chapter One," *True to Life Adventure Stories, Volume Two,* edited by Judy Grahn (Trumansburg, New York: Crossing Press, 1981).
"Shoes," *True to Life Adventure Stories, Volume One*, edited by Judy Grahn (Trumansburg, New York: Crossing Press, 1983): 176-83.

[Also published in *I Never Told Anyone* edited by Ellen Bass and Louise Thornton (New York: Harper and Row, 1985)].

"Revolution: It's Not Neat or Pretty or Quick," *This Bridge Called My Back: Writings by Radical Women of Color*, edited by Cherríe Moraga and Gloria Anzaldúa (New York: Kitchen Table: Women of Color Press, 1983): 238-42.

"Poetry at Women's Music Festivals: Oil and Water," *Hot Wire* 2, number 4 (November 1986): 52, 53, 63.

"Gay Parenting, Or, Look Out, Anita," *Politics of the Heart: A Lesbian Parenting Anthology*, edited by Sandra Pollack and Jeanne Vaughn (Ithaca, New York: Firebrand, 1987): 94-99.

"On Stage and Off: 1987 March on Washington," *Hot Wire* 5, number 1 (January 1989): 16, 17, 58.

## RECORDED WORK

"Any Woman's Blues," anthology. Unitarian Service Committee, 1975.

"Lesbian Concentrate," anthology. *Olivia Records*. 1977.

"Where Would I Be Without You: The Poetry of Pat Parker and Judy Grahn." *Olivia Records*. 1976.

## Interviews

Jane, Jessie. "Lord! What Kind of Child Is This." *Gay Community News* (May 31, 1975): 10.

Rushin, Kate. "Pat Parker: Creating Room to Speak and Grow." *Sojourner* 11 (October 1985): 28-29.

Woodwoman, Libby. "Pat Parker Talks About Her Life and Her Work." *Margins* (August 1975): 60-61.

## CRITICAL WRITING ABOUT PARKER

Ali, Kazim. "The Killer Will Remain Free: On Pat Parker and the Poetics of Madness." *Journal of Lesbian Studies* 19, no. 3 (Fall 2015): 379-383.

Annas, Pamela. "A Poetry of Survival: Unmaking and Renaming in the Poetry of Audre Lorde, Pat Parker, Sylvia Plath, and Adrienne Rich." *Colby Library Quarterly* 18 (March 1982): 9-25.

Beemyn, Brett. "Bibliography of Works by and about Pat Parker (1944-1989)," *SAGE* VI, no. 1 (Summer 1989): 81.

Callaghan, Dympna. "Pat Parker: Feminism in Postmodernity" in *Contemporary Poetry Meets Modern Theory*, ed. Antony Easthope and John O. Thompson (University of Toronto Press, 1991).

Clarke, Cheryl. Review of *Movement in Black*, (*Conditions: Six*, 1980): 217-225.

Clarke, Cheryl and Julie R. Enszer. "Introduction: Where Would I Be Without You." *Journal of Lesbian Studies* 19, no. 3 (Summer 2015): 275-289.

Clay, Andreana. "Yearnings and Other "Acts of Perversion": Or Where Would I Be Without Lesbian Drumming?" *Journal of Lesbian Studies* 19, no. 3 (Summer 2015): 384-399.

Folayan, Ayofemi, and Stephania Byrd. "Pat Parker" in *Contemporary Lesbian Writers of the United States: A Bio-Bibliographical Critical Sourcebook*, ed. Sandra Pollack and Denise D. Knight (Greenwood, 1993).

Green, Jr., David B. "'Anything That Gets Me in My Heart': Pat Parker's Poetry of Justice." *Journal of Lesbian Studies* 19, no. 3 (Summer 2015): 317-335.

Garber, Linda. Identity Poetics: Race, Class, and the Lesbian Feminist Roots of Queer Theory (Columbia University Press, 2001).

Kuras, Pat. "Pat Parker: Poet as Preacher" (*Gay Community News*, 1985).

Moraga, Cherríe. *A Xicana Codex of Changing Consciousness: Writings 2000-2010*. (Duke University Press, 2011).

Smith, Barbara. "Naming the Unnameable: The Poetry of Pat Parker." *Conditions: Three* (Spring 1976): 99-103.

Van Ausdall, Mimi Iimuro. "'The Day All of the Different Parts of Me Can Come Along': Intersectionality and U.S. Third World Feminism in the Poetry of Pat Parker and Willyce Kim. *Journal of Lesbian Studies* 19, no. 3 (Summer 2015): 336-356.

Warner, Sara. *Acts of Gaiety: LGBT Performance and the Politics of Pleasure* (University of Michigan Press, 2012).

Washburn, Amy. "Unpacking Pat Parker: Intersections and Revolutions in "Movement in Black"." *Journal of Lesbian Studies* 19, no. 3 (Summer 2015): 305-316.

# Appendix: Tables of Contents

*Child of Myself* (San Lorenzo, CA: Shameless Hussy Press, 1971)

**Dedication:**

This book is dedicated
to my father, who compromised
his dreams that I might realize mine.

**Table of Contents**

> [from cavities of bone]
> Goat Child
> [With the sun]*
> Ice Cream Blues**
> Fuller Brush Day
> [Sometimes my husband]
> For Donna
> Assassination**
> [Brother]
> [Move in darkness]
> [To see a may cry]
> [You can't be sure of anything these days]
> Exodus
> For Michael on his third birthday
> A Family Tree
> Dialogue
> A Moment Left Behind
> [Let me come to you naked]

\* [With the sun] is later titled by Parker "Desire."
\** "Ice Cream Blues" and "Assassination" were not included in the second edition of *Child of Myself* from the Women's Press Collective.

**Child of Myself** (Oakland, CA: Women's Press Collective, 1972, 1974)

**Table of Contents**

[from cavities of bone]
[Brother]
[Sometimes my husband]
Fuller Brush Day
Fuller Brush 2
[To see a may cry]
[You can't be sure of anything these days]
Exodus
[In English Lit.,]
[My heart is fresh cement,]
For Michael on his third birthday
For Donna
Dialogue
A Family Tree
Goat Child
A Moment Left Behind
[Move in darkness]
[love]
Autumn Morning
[With the sun]*
From Deep Within
[Let me come to you naked]

* [With the sun] is later titled by Parker "Desire."

***Pit Stop*** (Oakland, CA: Women's Press Collective, 1973, 1975)

## Table of Contents

* This poem is not included in later iterations of *Movement in Black*; it is restored in this edition.

***Womanslaughter*** (Oakland, CA: Diana Press, Inc., 1978)

**Table of Contents**

All of the poems of *Womanslaughter* are included in *Movement in Black*, some poems have different titles; some poems are edited.

# A Midsummer Night's Press

**A Midsummer Night's Press** was founded by Lawrence Schimel in New Haven, CT in 1991. Using a letterpress, it published broadsides of poems by Nancy Willard, Joe Haldeman, and Jane Yolen, among others, in signed, limited editions of 126 copies, numbered 1-100 and lettered A-Z. In 1993, the publisher moved to New York and the press went on hiatus until 2007, when it began publishing perfect-bound, commercially-printed books, under the imprints:

## Fabula Rasa

**Fabula Rasa**: devoted to works inspired by mythology, folklore, and fairy tales. Titles from this imprint include *Fairy Tales for Writers* by Lawrence Schimel, *Fortune's Lover: A Book of Tarot Poems* by Rachel Pollack, *Fairy Tales in Electri-city* by Francesca Lia Block, *The Last Selchie Child* by Jane Yolen, *What If What's Imagined Were All True* by Roz Kaveney, and *Lilith's Demons* by Julie R. Enszer.

## Body Language

**Body Language**: devoted to texts exploring questions of gender and sexual identity. Titles from this imprint include *This is What Happened in Our Other Life* by Achy Obejas, *Banalities* by Brane Mozetic (translated from the Slovene by Elizabeta Zargi with Timothy Liu), *Handmade Love* by Julie R. Enszer, *Mute* by Raymond Luczak; *Milk and Honey: A Celebration of Jewish Lesbian Poetry* edited by Julie R. Enszer, *Dialectic of the Flesh* by Roz Kaveney, *Fortunate Light* by David Bergman, *Deleted Names* by Lawrence Schimel, *This Life Now* by Michael Broder, and *When I Was Straight* by Julie Marie Wade.

## Periscope

**Periscope**: devoted to works of poetry in translation by women writers. The first titles are: *One is None* by Estonian poet Kätlin Kaldmaa (translated by Miriam McIlfatrick), *Anything Could Happen* by Slovenian poet Jana Putrle (translated by Barbara Jursa), and *Dissection* by Spanish poet Care Santos (translated by Lawrence Schimel).

# Sinister Wisdom

*Sinister Wisdom* is a multicultural lesbian literary & art journal that publishes four issues each year. Publishing since 1976, *Sinister Wisdom* works to create a multicultural, multi-class lesbian space. *Sinister Wisdom* seeks to open, consider and advance the exploration of community issues. *Sinister Wisdom* recognizes the power of language to reflect our diverse experiences and to enhance our ability to develop critical judgment, as lesbians evaluating our community and our world.

Editor and Publisher: Julie R. Enszer, PhD.

Board of Directors: Tara Shea Burke, Cheryl Clarke, Kathleen DeBold, Julie R. Enszer, Sue Lenaerts, Joan Nestle, Rose Norman, Judith K. Witherow.

Statements made and opinions expressed in this publication do not necessarily reflect the views of the publisher, board members, or editor(s) of *Sinister Wisdom*.

Former editors and publishers:
>Harriet Ellenberger (aka Desmoines)
>>and Catherine Nicholson (1976-1981)
>Michelle Cliff and Adrienne Rich (1981-1983)
>Michaele Uccella (1983-1984)
>Melanie Kaye/Kantrowitz (1983-1987)
>Elana Dykewomon (1987-1994)
>Caryatis Cardea (1991-1994)
>Akiba Onada-Sikwoia (1995-1997)
>Margo Mercedes Rivera-Weiss (1997-2000)
>Fran Day (2004-2010)
>Julie R. Enszer & Merry Gangemi (2010-2013)
>Julie R. Enszer (2013- )

Subscribe online: www.SinisterWisdom.org

Join *Sinister Wisdom* on Facebook: www.Facebook.com/SinisterWisdom
*Sinister Wisdom* is a U.S. non-profit organization; donations to support the work and distribution of *Sinister Wisdom* are welcome and appreciated.

Consider including *Sinister Wisdom* in your will.

# Sapphic Classics

The Sapphic Classics series, copublished by *Sinister Wisdom* and A Midsummer Night's Press, reprints iconic works of lesbian poetry in new editions with original introductions and afterwords to help bring these important works to new generations of readers.

The previous titles in this annual series are:

*Crime Against Nature* by Minnie Bruce Pratt
*Living as a Lesbian* by Cheryl Clarke
*What Can I Ask: New and Selected Poems* by Elana Dykewomon